ANASAZI POTTERY

Maxwell Museum of Anthropology
Publication Series

GENERAL EDITORS:

J. J. Brody
Mari Lyn Salvador

ANASAZI POTTERY

TEN CENTURIES OF PREHISTORIC CERAMIC ART
in the
FOUR CORNERS COUNTRY
of the
SOUTHWESTERN UNITED STATES

as illustrated by
THE EARL H. MORRIS MEMORIAL POTTERY COLLECTION
in the
UNIVERSITY OF COLORADO MUSEUM

by

Robert H. Lister and Florence C. Lister

Published by the

MAXWELL MUSEUM OF ANTHROPOLOGY

and the

UNIVERSITY OF NEW MEXICO PRESS
Albuquerque

Manufactured in the United States of America.
Library of Congress Catalog Card Number 78-6825.
International Standard Book Number 0-8263-0473-7.
Sixth printing 1990

PREFACE

Following the death in 1956 of the distinguished Southwestern archaeologist Earl Morris, the University of Colorado acquired his collection of artifacts, library, and personal papers. Using these materials, and aided by information obtained from his associates and fellow archaeologists, we compiled and published his biography.

Our book, although noting Earl's obsession for collecting prehistoric pottery, did not attempt to describe his personal collection. Once the collection was analyzed, however, its significance for illustrating the ceramic artistry of the ancient Anasazi became apparent. Furthermore, the comments Earl wrote about his pots are of interest and historical value. This volume has been prepared, therefore, to describe an outstanding achievement in ceramic art and to tell something of the man who did so much to contribute to its recognition.

Earl Morris was a graduate of the University of Colorado, but his archaeological competence was acquired primarily through his own digging experiences, although he did a few short stints as an apprentice under several well known archaeologists. Earl is best known as a Southwestern archaeologist, but he spent several seasons in the Maya area of Middle America with Carnegie Institution expeditions during the latter part of his career. It was in the Southwest, particularly the country drained by the San Juan River, that Earl did the vast majority of his archaeological research, and it was a fortunate combination of his inquisitive mind, his outstanding ability as a field archaeologist, his perseverance, and his almost uncanny knack of analyzing and usually solving complicated practical and theoretical problems that allowed him to make a great many significant contributions to Southwestern archaeology during its formative years. His Southwestern explorations and excavations were sponsored by the School of American Archaeology, the Carnegie Institution of Washington, the American Museum of Natural History, and the University of Colorado Museum. On numerous occasions he led expeditions under joint auspices of the University of Colorado Museum and one of these other institutions. As he successively assumed more important positions in these organizations, he seems always to have retained a sentimental tie with the University of Colorado Museum. As a conse-

quence of this interest and his extensive excavations over many years, he built up an outstanding assortment of prehistoric pottery in the Museum. The addition of his private collection to this assemblage has given the University of Colorado Museum one of the most representative collections of Anasazi pottery in any museum. Earl Morris was awarded a variety of honors, medals and academic degrees, but the fact that most of his colleagues and coworkers respectfully referred to him as the best "dirt archaeologist" in the Southwest probably gave him greater personal satisfaction.

Many of the details of Morris' life, his important scientific achievements, and his bibliography are presented in our book, *Earl Morris and Southwestern Archaeology*. A synopsis of his activities with and contributions to the University of Colorado Museum, which extended from the time he entered the University in 1908 until his death in 1956, appears in a memorial issue of *Southwestern Lore*, journal of the Colorado Archaeological Society (Vol. XXII, No. 3, 1956).

Archaeology was Earl Morris' vocation, and archaeology was his avocation. When he was not participating in or directing scientific archaeological expeditions, which he did almost year around for most of his life, he found relaxation and personal satisfaction in searching for examples of ancient pottery. This study is concerned with some of the results of Earl's hobby.

We extend to the following individuals our sincere thanks for contributing to this volume or for providing assistance and services during its preparation. Hugo Rodeck, Director of the University of Colorado Museum, graciously made the Morris Collection available to us for study and photography. Museum staff members Joe Ben Wheat and Lowell Swenson have provided us much assistance. The late Daniel Houtz took the original photographs of the more important vessels in the collection; we deeply regret that he did not live to see this final product to which he so significantly contributed. Roger Luebbers has photographed the remainder of the specimens, and Paul Folse has assisted in the darkroom. Hannah Huse, Museum Assistant in Anthropology, has helped classify the pots, has measured them, and has provided us with other information about the collection from the Museum records. Her aid has been especially valuable.

CONTENTS

FIGURES

In pottery making Pueblo art found its highest expression. The gracefulness of contour, and the dignified simplicity of ornamentation to be observed in some of the specimens, make one realize that the search for beauty was as keenly alive in the hearts of prehistoric Southwestern peoples as it is in our own today. (Morris, 1917, p. 178)

INTRODUCTION

Earl Morris was a determined collector. He was known to hike tirelessly and scale perilous cliffs, to hazard driving miles over impossible roads, to dig like a machine for days in order to obtain another artifact. Most of this fierce urge for acquisition was focused upon prehistoric pottery of the San Juan River drainage of the Four Corners county—the area where the states of Arizona, Utah, Colorado, and New Mexico meet at a common point. The prehistoric Indian culture of that region was known as the Basket Maker-Pueblo tradition at one time since it was believed that two groups of Indians, each with a distinct culture pattern, were represented. Now, because the tradition has been demonstrated to be a continuum both physically and culturally the term Anasazi has been applied to it, although the names Basket Maker and Pueblo have been retained by some to designate stages within the sequence.

The deep abiding passion Earl felt for ancient pottery was at first inspired by the interest both his parents displayed in amassing assortments of vessels from the nearby ruins. His earliest memories of his father were of the view of Scott's broad back bent over a trench as he knocked free the hard adobe earth from a vessel wall as one might release a pan of jello from a mold. He recalled his mother carefully wrapping especially choice pots in soft towels before she packed them in a shabby satchel she kept at her feet during the frequent moves necessitated by her husband's work. He remembered the long conversations between his father and other men of the valley of the latest finds each had made. As a young boy he recalled with pleasure the family picnics to a ruin where there was productive digging, and in the grief of his father's death, he found such activity provided a much needed emotional outlet. Thus, by adolescence Earl had handled or seen more pottery from the San Juan valley about Farmington, New Mexico, than any other person, and it is safe to assume that he never forgot a detail of any of it. He had become a confirmed pothunter.

The thrill and challenge of the search heightened by the attainment of specimens were important to him as they were to other collectors. However, Earl went far beyond the point at which most antiquarians stalled. Through his education in school and in the field, he developed the keenest appreciation for the best, the aberrant, and the everyday products of San Juan potters. Through stylistic similiarities and differences and geographic locations he sought cultural overtones implicit in each pot.

Although many of his father's collections were sold and Earl himself sold or gave away several of his personal hoards, at the time of his death in 1956 he owned 361 vessels. Some had been received as gifts from friends who knew of his love of pottery. Others had been acquired through purchase or trade, usually after years of dickering. But most had been excavated by Earl.

In Earl's youth when hunting in the ruins was every man's sport, no one thought much of the boy's predilection for groveling about for pots except that it was an odd pastime for a youngster. However, in later years as the unlicensed search for relics became regarded as a sin against science, some archaeologists disapproved of such activity on Earl's part, even though they knew of his strict integrity about specimens secured under the auspices of various agencies. Few persons, however, had the heart to voice a protest because in the utter rapture with which a pot was greeted they saw justification. They knew of the loving care given his collection and the detailed record as to circumstances of obtainment. Furthermore, they viewed Earl's private excavations as an extension of his official activities for the University of Colorado Museum for often he expressed the anticipation that his private collection ultimately would be integrated into those he had made for that institution. This goal was realized posthumously when the Regents of the University of Colorado authorized acquisition of the Morris scientific library, personal papers, field notes, and the collection of artifacts. The collection and Morris' personal papers and notes are now housed in the University of Colorado Museum.

The vessels illustrated herein include all of the prehistoric specimens in the collection from the San Juan area and a few examples from other parts of the Southwest. Earl's research and collecting was focused upon the eastern San Juan, especially in, adjacent to, and between the Chaco Canyon and Mesa Verde areas. He did little work in the Kayenta area to the west. His collection reflects this circumstance as it consists mainly of specimens from the eastern San Juan and contains but few examples from the western sectors of the territory. A small number of fragmentary specimens and historic pots in the collection have been excluded from this study.

The vessels shown in larger size in the figures are the outstanding ones of the collection, not always notable because of the intrinsic worth of the pots themselves but sometimes because of the notes appended. The introductory section of the catalogue and the comments appearing with the photos were written by Earl. They tell much of the qualities of this great ceramic craft developed by the Anasazi women but, equally important here, they reveal the character of the man who held them in trust for future generations. Sometimes the notations throw light upon aspects of Anasazi culture other than ceramics. Following Morris' notes about each vessel, or group of vessels, dimensions of the specimens, modern typological classifications of them, and the University of Colorado Museum catalogue number of each are presented. In many instances our comments are appended to Earl's original statements. To aid in distinguishing between the two, Morris' words and ours are set in different types.

In many of the figures we have included photographs, in smaller size, of the additional examples of vessels in the collection that are similar in type, style, or age to those that are principally illustrated. The University of Colorado Museum catalogue number, the provenience, type, and size are listed; however, they are not depicted at a common scale, nor are Morris' comments about them included.

Because this extensive collection of pottery contains representatives of the various types of eastern San Juan pottery illustrative of the stages through which this prehistoric craft evolved, we have taken the liberty of rearranging the Morris catalogue so that specimens are placed in a general chronological and geographical order rather than in their original position in the listings. Items are arranged by the locality in which they were found rather than by their presumed place of manufacture. We have introduced statements at intervals outlining the development, in both form and decoration, of prehistoric Anasazi pottery of the eastern San Juan. Attention is called to the characteristics of the pottery of each culture period and the specializations that occurred in particular regions.

Among the examples illustrated from the San Juan, we have included one vessel that is not from the Morris Collection, a basket-molded dried mud container. The specimen is one of several collected by Morris in northeastern Arizona and deposited in the University of Colorado Museum. He had no examples of these crude bowls in his private collection, but since Earl believed that it might have been from such simple beginnings that Anasazi pottery making evolved (Morris, 1927) we have included an illustration of one of these vessels from the museum collections. Technically it is not pottery since it is unfired.

By starting with simple dried mud containers from the latter part of Basket Maker II, and continuing through the well-developed pottery of Pueblo III, a span of approximately ten centuries of prehistoric San Juan pottery development is illustrated by specimens from the Morris Collection. The large number of vessels in the assemblage and the fact that it contains more examples of the typical and ordinary kinds of pottery rather than the unusual or unique, make it a particularly valuable study collection. The examples of pottery from areas other than the San Juan are neither extensive nor representative of the sequences of ceramic development in those regions. They are included to demonstrate the areal differences, which reflect cultural variations, in prehistoric pottery making in the Southwest. The breadth of Earl's collecting activities also is shown by the widespread sources of these specimens.

The Pecos Classification, a system of taxonomy devised by archaeologists for listing successive stages of Anasazi culture and their diagnostic characteristics, has been employed as a chronological framework for the collection. In a general way the stages of the Pecos Classification may be dated as follows:

A.D.	100	200	300	400	500	600	700	800	900	1000	1100	1200	1300	1400	1500
		Basket Maker II			Basket Maker III			Pueblo I		Pueblo II		Pueblo III		Pueblo IV	

We usually have followed the classificatory schemes of Abel (1955), Colton (1955, 1956), Rohn (1959), and Hayes (1964) in typing the pots in the collection. However, we have employed certain modifications, particularly in dealing with San Juan gray and red wares and in designating periods of manufacture of a few types. These modifications have resulted from our analyses of pottery from sites we have excavated in the Mesa Verde area. Our system of typology has been described in reports upon our Mesa Verde investigations (Lister, 1964: 47-56; 1965: 62-65; 1966: 88-91). Hayes' publication (1964: 42-75) contains the most up-to-date description of many of the types of pottery included in the Morris Collection. Florence Lister (Lister and Lister, 1961: 32-90) has published a comprehensive discussion of San Juan ceramics which emphasizes the basic similiarities of wares throughout the entire region between Basket Maker III and Pueblo II times. Local specialization, which can be easily noted in such subareas as Chaco Canyon, Kayenta, and Mesa Verde, took place primarily during Pueblo III.

AUTHORS' NOTE:

Anasazi Pottery is a slightly revised version of the volume entitled *The Earl H. Morris Memorial Pottery Collection*, published in 1969 by the University of Colorado Press as No. 16 in their Series in Anthropology. Since the original edition of this work appeared, a revision of technical descriptions of pottery types found in and about Mesa Verde has been published:

BRETERNITZ, DAVID A., ARTHUR H. ROHN, JR. AND ELIZABETH A. MORRIS (COMPILERS)
    1974 "Prehistoric Ceramics of the Mesa Verde Region." *Museum of Northern Arizona Ceramic Series*, No. 5. Flagstaff.

This current, detailed treatment of Mesa Verde pottery is an important addition to the literature on Southwest pottery (see Bibliography, p. 94).

Many of the illustrations used in *Anasazi Pottery* are included in *Prehistoric Ceramics of the Mesa Verde Region* to exemplify the several types of pottery described in that monograph. Compilers of that volume have chosen to use the name Deadmans Black-on-red for the type that is labeled here as La Plata Black-on-red. They do note, however, that in most publications the type has been called La Plata Black-on-red. Furthermore, some of the vessels identified here as La Plata Black-on-white actually may be Chapin Black-on-white as defined in *Prehistoric Ceramics of the Mesa Verde Region*. The difference between the two types is in the type of temper employed in the paste of the vessels. Identification of temper is not always possible when dealing with whole vessels such as those in the Morris collection.

R.H.L.
F.C.L.
1978

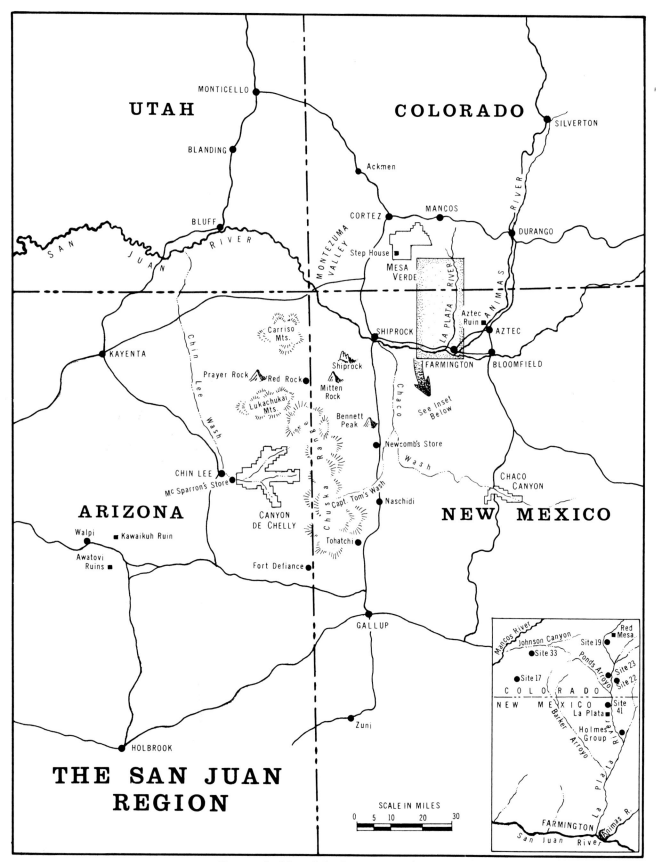

FIGURE 1. Map of the San Juan Region.

CATALOGUE OF THE ARCHAEOLOGICAL COLLECTION
OF EARL H. MORRIS (1956)

As a beginning of the catalogue of my archaeological collection, it might be excusable to make a historical statement that, although of no particular importance, might be of interest to some. In the summer of 1891 my father, Scott N. Morris, had been freighting ore from the mines at Rico, Colorado. When snow closed the roads that fall, he decided to winter his stock at Farmington, New Mexico. The Animas and San Juan valleys were sparsely settled at that time, but a good part of the land that had been brought under irrigation had been planted to alfalfa; hence hay was cheap. On the way down, my father paused in Durango, Colorado, to lay in supplies for the winter. He had picked up a good deal of information about the Farmington country and knew that there were many ruins scattered along the valley. In talking with a group of men in Kruche's Shoe Store in Durango, he said that he intended to do some digging during the winter. A gentleman stepped up and presented his card, saying, "I would like to have the first chance to purchase any relics that you find this winter." It was Gilbert McClurg of Colorado Springs. Both he and his wife, Virginia McClurg, were well-known lecturers at that time.

Arrived in Farmington, Father found great difficulty in securing a house in which to live. There were only about half a dozen buildings in the town then, and although the ranchers had roofs of sorts over their own heads, they had none to spare. Finally Father located an ex-slave, Albert Wooton by name, who was a renter on what was known as the Kehoe place, although owned by S. R. Blake. Uncle Albert, as we called him, whitewashed his chicken coop, moved into it himself, and let us have his adobe house. This house was situated near the brink of the mesa about a mile southwest of the center of the town of Farmington, overlooking the swampy river valley of the Animas to the east. On the very edge of the declivity, within a stone's throw of the house, was a good-sized mound marking the remains of a small cobblestone pueblo.

The Coolidge Canal, which irrigates the Kirtland-Fruitland district, was under construction. Father got his teams on the job under a foreman so that his own time was largely free. He had talked a good deal with the local settlers about his intention to do some digging, and they all regarded it as a foolish notion because they said no one had found any unbroken pottery in that part of the country. The reason would seem to have been that none of them had dug in a definite search for pottery, and what they had turned up in breaking land for cultivation naturally had been shattered by the plow.

Father started a drift through the mound in the door yard. According to my mother's account, many times repeated to me, he worked six days without finding anything more than a few stone tools. Then, just at sundown one afternoon, he broke through a wall, and on the other side, no more than a span beneath the surface, he struck a small stone slab covering the mouth of what I now know to have been a Mesa Verde mug. When darkness fell, he went on by lantern light and before morning had taken out 40 pottery vessels, many of them unbroken. He had gotten into a burial room where the bodies lay, at least in places, three deep.

This find stimulated others to begin digging. Conspicuous among these were the Brown brothers, who lived on the road to Durango, about a mile and a half east of Farmington.

By spring Father had exhumed quite a collection himself, had secured what the Brown brothers had dug up, and had traded horse gear for what a group of cowboys who had wintered at Navajo or Cottonwood Springs had scratched out during their spare time. He also acquired, either by trade or purchase, the specimens found by one De Luche, a settler in the Fruitland valley. On the way back to the mines Father displayed his collection in Durango and wired Mr. McClurg that it was subject to his inspection. At the same time McLloyd and Graham had brought in their first collection from the Grand Gulch country. They were rather contemptuous of Father's display because it contained only pottery and objects of bone and stone whereas their own consisted of perishable materials, including a considerable collection of "mummies." They were somewhat astonished when Mr. McClurg, who came posthaste, purchased my father's collection in preference to their own. My mother told me that there were 160 pieces of unbroken pottery in this collection. It eventually became the property of the Taylor Museum in Colorado Springs. I have seen what remains of it there, but feel certain that before the collection reached the museum a considerable part of it had been otherwise disposed of.

The winter of 1892 saw Father again in Farmington. This time we lived in a little log cabin on the edge of a hill about two miles east of town, on what was then known as the Rogers' ranch. This adjoined the homestead of the Brown brothers on the east. Later it passed into the hands of Shidler, then into those of Weightman, and finally became the property of Phil Schenk, one of the large apple producers of the Farmington district at the present time.

There was a good-sized ruin where Schenk's dwelling and store houses now (1942) stand, and there were other mounds all up and down the terrace. Father spent a fair part of the winter digging in these, and as a result of his own activities, as well as trade and purchase, he amassed during the winter a collection which he sold to the Carnegie Library Association of Pittsburgh. I have never looked up this collection, so do not know where it is housed, but I do have some photographs of it that will be accounted for at some point in the catalogue. It must have been that this collection was not sold immediately. Where it may have been kept until the following winter, I have no idea, but I know from my own memory that we had it in the house on the mesa edge, overlooking Farmington from the north, which Father bought from June Roberts in the fall of 1893. In early winter of that year a Mr. Hill, then owner of mines near Silverton, and his nephew, an architect named Orth, came down and accompanied my father on a trip to Chaco Canyon. It was quite a trek in those days, some 75 miles across country where the only roads were Indian horse trails—Navajo had few wagons at that time. The trip was made in four-horse freight wagons. Owing to the scarcity of feed and the necessity of melting snow at most of their stops to water the stock, no great amount of digging was done. However, my father and his teamsters cut the first drifts through the great refuse piles of Pueblo Bonito on the expectation that they would contain burials as did the trash mounds of the small ruins with which Father was familiar. They brought back only a few specimens, but Mr. Orth secured excellent photographs of most of the large ruins along the Chaco and made a map of their locations. I know that the 1892 collection was retained until after the trip to the Chaco, because among the photographs of it there is a section of a pole-and-plank ceiling which was taken from one of the Chaco pueblos. I presume it was in the spring of 1894 that this collection was sent to Pittsburgh.

For nearly a decade after 1894 my father had little opportunity to dig. We were gone from the country most of the time, he following whatever work he could find for his teams—the construction of the Trout Lake dam, between Telluride and Rico; lumbering and tie cutting in the Cloudcroft country of southern New Mexico; railroad construction of the line that was building from El Paso to White Oaks; and railroad building in the Cherokee and Osage districts of Indian territory. Finally, in 1903, Father having sold his grading outfit, we returned to Farmington, and he repurchased our previous home, which had been lost under a mortage foreclosure.

During the following year Father and I dug a good deal, mostly in the ruins on the Blake ranch on the mesa overlooking the bottoms of the San Juan just southwest of Farmington. My father was killed in December of 1904, but throughout the following year I put in my spare time among the ruins that could be reached on foot from Farmington. Most of the collection begun by my father and myself in 1904 and added to by me as time went on eventually was sold to the American Museum of Natural History in 1916, when I needed money to complete the year I spent at Columbia University.

From the very beginning my mother began to select out certain pieces of pottery that particularly caught her fancy. Those from the early collections she carted about with her from place to place, and that they escaped breakage during our many journeys speaks well for the care she took of them. I continued Father's practice of giving her any she wanted from the specimens that I found, and the material that she thus segregated is the nucleus of the collection to be covered by this catalogue.

FIGURE 2. Dipper bowl; first pot found by Morris.

SAN JUAN VALLEY, NEW MEXICO (FIGURE 2)

Small, nondescript black-on-white dipper bowl. The first piece of pottery found by me. It came from the ruin on the Rogers' ranch where the house of Phil Schenk now stands. Some time in the winter of 1892 and '93 my father, to get me out from under his feet, shortened the handle of a nearly wornout pick and told me to get over in that hole he had dug the day before to do some digging for myself. I climbed into it, whacked the bank with the pick, and out rolled what I supposed was a cobblestone until I noticed the stub of a handle on one side. It was a surprise to everyone that the Three-year-old had found a piece of pottery; so Father took me and the dipper bowl across the road to our cabin to exhibit us to Mother. She came back with us to see where the find had been made, and with her butcher knife dug out the skull of the burial to which the dipper bowl belonged.

Dimensions: Height, 1⅞ in. (4.9 cm.).
                Maximum diameter, 3¾ in. (9.4 cm.).
Type: McElmo Black-on-white.
UCM No. 9311.

Comments: This piece of pottery is of historic interest since it is the first specimen collected by Earl Morris.

Figure 3. San Juan, Basket Maker II; unfired mud container.

BASKET MAKER II

NAVAJO RESERVATION, ARIZONA (FIGURE 3)

(*Top,* Exterior view; *Bottom,* Side view.) Mud bowl with lugs. Extremely asymmetrical. Basket which served as mold was rather tray-shaped. Apparently it was old and distorted from use since the stitch impressions fade out toward the bottom, while the rise on one side is steep and on the other pronouncedly gentle and flaring. The free rim that was modeled on above the basket edge grades from 1⅝ inches in width on the steep side to 3⅛ inches on the flaring one. On one side of the bowl the builder spread only ¼ inch of clay against the basket, thus imparting to that area a thinness totally impractical for a container of such size. After removal from the mold and probably after drying had caused cracks to develop that reached entirely through the wall, the area in question was reinforced by smearing a thick patch of clay against the exterior, portions of which later scaled off to reveal the basket impression beneath. In other places the constriction left by the basket rim cuts the wall to a thickness of ¼ inch while the base of the free rim immediately above juts outward to a total thickness of almost ½ inch. The margin is round and wavy. The interior of the bowl is abraded by use to the obliteration of the original finish, except just below the rim, where irregular more or less horizontal smoothing strokes may still be traced. The whole expanse is undulating as a result of the pinching pressure which joined the structural units. Along one arc, failure to pinch them well together shows the free rim to have been built up of strips of clay laid horizontally with downward and outward shingle-like overlap. The ultimate finish of the exterior of the free rim was the result of vigorous stroking for the most part parallel to the margin with an uneven-edged tool which usually tended to level down the irregularities, but sometimes deeply scored the surface.

The opposing lugs are inserted practically halfway between the top of the mold and the margin. They are carelessly modeled flat plates of clay narrowing to rounded ends. They slant downward, one much more than the other. Molds of shreds of juniper bark temper are very plentiful. The interior surface of the vessel checked badly in drying. Accidental firing burned a portion of one side to a light brick red, and slightly warped some of the fragments.

Dimensions: Height, 5⅛ in. (12.8 cm.).
Maximum diameter, 15⅛ in. (38 cm.).
Type: Unfired mud container.
UCM No. 19687.

Comments: This mud container is one of a collection of 25 recovered by Morris in 1931 from Broken Flute Cave in the Red Rocks Valley on the Navajo Reservation. In these works of clay Morris saw what he felt was further support for his theory of the origin of San Juan pottery that he had first formulated after finding unfired clay vessels in a Basket Maker II context in Canyon del Muerto (Morris, 1927). His concept was that pottery-making in the San Juan could be evolved through a series of steps: (1) adding mud liners to bowl- or tray-shaped baskets when they were used in parching seeds; (2) using thick basket-molded, fiber-tempered mud bowls, usually with a heightening rim added above the edge of the basket and lugs attached to the exterior, as containers for dry commodities; (3) the accidental burning of one of these mud containers demonstrating that the firing of clay would make it impervious to water; (4) and finally, making true pottery by purposely firing vessels modeled of clay.

Today, most archaeologists favor the notion that pottery-making was introduced into the American Southwest from Mexico as one of a series of cultural influences from the south. The Mogollon culture, which centers in the mountains of southeastern Arizona and southwestern New Mexico, is believed to have received pottery from Mexican sources as early as 100 B.C. The Anasazi are thought to have obtained it through diffusion from the Mogollon sometime around A.D. 300 or 400.

BASKET MAKER III

DURANGO, COLORADO (FIGURE 4)

(*Left.*) Black-on-white bowl. Impressions of coiled basket around exterior. This badly eroded specimen is of particular interest because the pattern consists of an encircling row of 12 human figures, one set of alternates wearing what clearly seems to be the Hopi maiden's squash-blossom headdress; the other set having a single device which seems to be a great feather rising from the left side of the head to slope across it to the right. The hands of the figures are joined, and the feet may have rested on a basal line. The pattern has been somewhat strengthened. Found by Frank Lee in the northwest edge of Durango, Colorado. Given to me in 1939.

Dimensions: Height, 3½ in. (9.1 cm.).
                Maximum diameter, 7¼ in. (18.4 cm.).
Type: La Plata Black-on-white.
UCM No. 9578.

Comments: Morris was of the opinion that the bases of many Basket Maker III globular-shaped vessels, or pots with bowl-like bottoms, were shaped or supported during construction by a mold—normally a coiled basket. Usually in the subsequent smoothing process an effort was made to obliterate the mold impression, but in many cases telltale stitch marks may be detected on the exteriors of vessels.

(*Middle.*) Bird-shaped vessel with secondary orifice in tail end.

Dimensions: Height, 2¾ in. (7.1 cm.).
                Length, 4 in. (10.2 cm.).
Type: Chapin Gray.
UCM No. 9574.

Comments: Small vessels similar in shape to the body of a plump bird are fairly frequent in Basket Maker III sites. The purpose of the secondary orifice in some, such as in this specimen, is not understood.

(*Right.*) Black-on-white bowl.

Both the bird-shaped vessel, described above, and this bowl were found near Durango, Colorado, and were given to me by I. F. Flora; I think it was in 1937.

Dimensions: Height, 3⅞ in. (10 cm.).
                Maximum diameter, 7⅛ in. (18.1 cm.).
Type: La Plata Black-on-white.
UCM No. 9573.

Comments: Lower part of Figure 4 is an enlargement of part of the design on the bowl in the upper left (UCM No. 9578).

FIGURE 4. San Juan, Basket Maker III; bowls and bird-shaped vessel.

9479

9557

9420

9335

Figure 5. San Juan, Basket Maker III; bird-shaped vessels, bowls.

Basket Maker III

La Plata, Colorado-New Mexico (Figure 5)

(*Left.*) Tiny Black-on-white bowl. A cylindrical stub handle about 1 inch long juts downward from one side, about ¾ inch below the rim. Found by Clint Wagner at a site on the east side of the La Plata valley, about a mile south of the Colorado line. Purchased from him, summer of 1934.

Dimensions: Height, 1¾ in. (4.6 cm.).
Maximum diameter, 3¾ in. (9.7 cm.).
Type: La Plata Black-on-white.
UCM No. 9570.

(*Middle.*) Black-on-white bowl. I found this with burials at Site 19, La Plata valley, fall of 1934.

Dimensions: Height, 3⅜ in. (8.6 cm.).
Maximum diameter, 5½ in. (14 cm.).
Type: La Plata Black-on-white.
UCM No. 9559.

(*Right.*) Very large bird-shaped vessel. Pierced lugs in wing positions; the once protuberant tail broken off. Once had a coat of fugitive red paint. Was with a burial of an adult at the center of a pile of gravel thrown out in the process of construction of a subterranean room well toward the south end of Site 23, La Plata valley, spring of 1928.

Dimensions: Height, 5¼ in. (13.5 cm.).
Length, 6⅛ in. (15.5 cm.).
Width, 4½ in. (11.3 cm.).
Type: Chapin Gray.
UCM No. 9557.

Comments: During Basket Maker III times, fugitive red paint, an impermanent wash of red ocher (hematite) placed on the pot after firing, was common practice in all sections of the San Juan. It was used mainly upon the exterior of plain gray vessels, to a lesser degree on decorated vessel exteriors. In certain parts of the San Juan, fugitive red continued as a decorative device into Pueblo II times.

Lower part of Figure 5 illustrates additional bird-shaped vessels in the Morris Collection. Those pictured are:

UCM No.	Provenience	Type	Height
9479	Near Farmington	Mancos B/W	2½ in. (6.3 cm.)
9557	La Plata valley	Chapin Gray	5¼ in. (13.5 cm.)
9420	La Plata valley	Mancos B/W	3⅝ in. (9.3 cm.)
9335	Near Farmington	McElmo B/W	4⅝ in. (11.8 cm.)

9562

FIGURE 6. San Juan, Basket Maker III; muffin-shaped vessels, bowl, canteen.

BASKET MAKER III

LA PLATA, COLORADO-NEW MEXICO (FIGURE 6)

(*Left.*) Muffin-shaped vessel with lateral spout. A large example of its kind. With the burial of an adult at the center of a heap of gravel thrown out in the process of construction of a subterranean room well toward the south end of Site 23, La Plata valley, spring of 1928.

Dimensions: Height, 3¼ in. (8.4 cm.).
Length, with spout, 5⅞ in. (15 cm.).
Type: Chapin Gray.
UCM No. 9558.

Comments: Small vessels with a hollow tube jutting from one side are a form characteristic of Basket Maker III. Nothing has been found to suggest what their purpose may have been.

(*Middle.*) Black-on-white bowl (illustrated in Morris, 1919, plate 65c). Heavy coat of fugitive red paint on exterior. This is the first Basket Maker III vessel I ever found or saw, summer of 1913. From Site 22, La Plata valley. About 1939 I secured it in exchange from the University of Colorado Museum.

Dimensions: Height, 4 in. (10.1 cm.).
Maximum diameter, 7¼ in. (18.5 cm.).
Type: La Plata Black-on-white.
UCM No. 9555.

(*Right.*) Double-necked canteen (illustrated in Morris, 1939, plate 192b). Plowed up by George Morgan on the mesa point between the La Plata River and Johnny Pond's Arroyo. Purchased in 1927.

Dimensions: Height, 5⅛ in. (13.1 cm.).
Maximum diameter, 5 in. (12.8 cm.).
Type: Chapin Gray.
UCM No. 9568.

Comments: This is a rather unique specimen. The custom of placing two necks on a canteen-shaped pot was never a common practice. The vessel is an orange-gray ware. Normally, the canteen has a globular or pear-shaped body, a short neck with small mouth, and two horizontally pierced lugs or eyelets to receive a cord for suspension. The form was never common, but became most frequent in Pueblo III.

A second muffin-shaped vessel with lateral spout and another view of the double-necked canteen illustrated on upper right are shown in the lower part of Figure 6. The muffin-shaped vessel is described as follows:

UCM No.	Provenience	Type	Height
9562	La Plata valley	Chapin Gray	2¾ in. (7 cm.)

Figure 7. San Juan, Basket Maker III; bowl.

Basket Maker III

Navajo Reservation, New Mexico (Figure 7)

Black-on-white bowl. In the years between 1923 and 1930, whenever I had any time to spare on trips across the reservation, I stopped to dig a bit somewhere along the line. I felt no compunction of conscience about this then, nor do I now. Sunday diggers from far and wide were looting the burial areas so rapidly that I considered it fully justified to prevent what I could from falling into their hands.

Obtained on one of these digging excursions was this bowl. Interior pattern an encircling row of 14 human figures holding hands and standing on a base line. Exterior of bottom smoothed to a diameter of about 4 inches. Has the appearance of unindented corrugations thence upward to the base of the half-inch rim. However, the coils are concentric instead of spiral. Heavy coat of fugitive red paint on exterior. From a site on the Tohatchi Flats, west of the Gallup-Shiprock highway.

Dimensions: Height, 3⅜ in. (8.7 cm.).
Maximum diameter, 7½ in. (19.1 cm.).
Type: La Plata Black-on-white.
UCM No. 9509.

Comments: Note the similarity between the pattern of human figures on this vessel and those on the bowl on the left in Figure 4. They were found about 110 miles apart. Highly geometricized life forms, including the human figure, occasionally were drawn by San Juan potters during Basket Maker III.

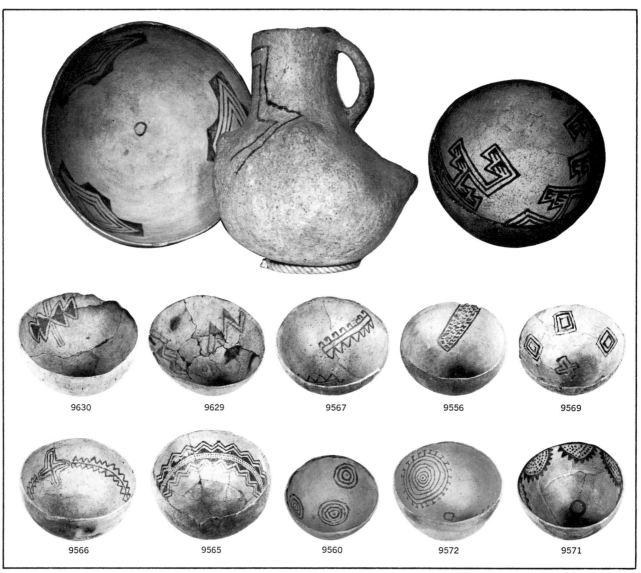

FIGURE 8. San Juan, Basket Maker III; bowls, bird-shaped vessel.

BASKET MAKER III

NAVAJO RESERVATION, ARIZONA-NEW MEXICO (FIGURE 8)

(*Left.*) Highly typical black-on-white bowl. Panel decoration on interior, with circle at center of bottom. Exterior bears impression of coiled basket mold and traces of fugitive red wash. Brought into Shiprock, New Mexico, by a Navajo, and given to me by Bruce Barnard in 1936.

Dimensions: Height, 3½ in. (8.9 cm.).
Maximum diameter, 6¾ in. (17.1 cm.).
Type: La Plata Black-on-white.
UCM No. 9462.

(*Middle.*) Bird-form pitcher. Two-strand vertical loop handle. Nodes in tail and wing positions, another at front of breast. Entire exterior retains traces of fugitive red wash. In addition, across the front of the neck and extending down in a zigzag on to the body are two parallel lines in black, obviously drawn over the red wash. This is the only Basket Maker III vessel that I have seen on which a surface treated with fugitive red has also been embellished with black. Secured from a Navajo who found it at a site on the Tohatchi Flats west of the Gallup-Shiprock highway.

Dimensions: Height, 6¾ in. (17.1 cm.).
Maximum diameter, 5⅝ in. (14.4 cm.).
Type: La Plata Black-on-white.
UCM No. 9510.

Comments: Morris (1927: 197) has gone to some length to show that the earliest pottery decorations were taken over directly from the preexistent art of basketry. Aside from an occasional life form, the patterns are in all cases geometric and predominately rectilinear. He states that some designs recur with sufficient frequency to show that they were not the creation of an individual decorator, but were devices familiar to the group as a whole. Most conspicuous of such designs are the rectangular panel with fringed or dentate margins, the zigzag encircling band, "spiral radii," the outlined cross, and the circle or rectangle with a row of short heavy T-shaped elements extending radially from the periphery. The basic elements in these designs are few: the line, more often straight than curved, usually solid, occasionally dotted; the dot-filled space; the basket stitch; the triangle, plain or fringed, sometimes used singly, sometimes in multiple arrangement; the terrace (rare); and the heavy T-shaped figure (Morris, 1939: 155).

Lower part of Figure 8 illustrates ten additional examples of La Plata Black-on-white bowls in the collection. Those pictured are:

(*Right.*) Black-on-white bowl. One of the finest examples of its kind in existence. The vessel is beautifully formed. The surface is true, but grainy. The rim line and opposing panels of decoration are in a jet black iron paint. The decoration would appear to be a direct copy from one of the finer contemporary baskets. The vessel is representative of the iron paint strain of Basket Maker III which occurs sporadically, apparently as trade ware around Durango, Colorado, is fairly prevalent in the La Plata valley, and is characteristic in the caves of the Prayer Rock district in northeastern Arizona. I found this in the extreme western end of the Mitten Rock group, summer of 1936. Accompanying the same skeleton with which the bowl was associated there had been a small squash pot, so many pieces of which had been dug away by a prairie dog that I did not attempt a restoration.

Dimensions: Height, 3⅛ in. (7.8 cm.).
Diameter at rim, 5⅜ in. (13.7 cm.).
Type: La Plata Black-on-white.
UCM No. 9579.

UCM No.	Provenience	Type	Diameter
9630	Mesa Verde	La Plata B/W	7½ in. (19.2 cm.)
9629	Mesa Verde	La Plata B/W	7 in. (17.8 cm.)
9567	La Plata valley	La Plata B/W	5¾ in. (14.7 cm.)
9556	La Plata valley	La Plata B/W	6¼ in. (15.9 cm.)
9569	La Plata valley	La Plata B/W	5⅛ in. (13.2 cm.)
9566	La Plata valley	La Plata B/W	6¾ in. (17.1 cm)
9565	La Plata valley	La Plata B/W	6½ in. (16.6 cm.)
9560	La Plata valley	La Plata B/W	5 in. (12.7 cm.)
9572	Holmes Group	La Plata B/W	6⅜ in. (16.2 cm.)
9571	Holmes Group	La Plata B/W	6⅛ in. (15.7 cm.)

9505

9533

9308

9469

FIGURE 9. San Juan, Basket Maker III-Pueblo I; bowl, jockey cap and half-gourd ladles.

BASKET MAKER III — PUEBLO I

NAVAJO RESERVATION, NEW MEXICO (FIGURE 9)

(*Left.*) Black-on-white bowl. Interior divided into quadrants, each of which bears drawings of human figures. Heavy coat of fugitive red paint on exterior. The bowl and the ladle in this illustration were secured from an Indian who obtained them from a site on the Tohatchi Flats, west of the Gallup-Shiprock highway.

Dimension: Height, 3⅝ in. (9.5 cm.).
Maximum diameter, 6¼ in. (16 cm.).
Type: La Plata Black-on-white.
UCM No. 9508.

(*Right.*) Jockey-cap ladle. The ladle deserves a word of comment. When it fell into my hands (secured from the Navajo Indians), the whole interior was leaden gray in color, and there were a number of dark splotches on the outside as well. I knew that the vessel would have been a good black-on-orange if fired as the maker intended it to be, and judged that the defects were due to under rather than to over-firing. After a long time I persuaded Miss Anna Shepard to lay aside her conscientious scruples and to refire it for me. It came out as clear and rich an example as I have ever seen of the early ware which Martin has tagged black-on-orange.

Dimensions: Height, 2⅝ in. (6.8 cm.).
Length, 6 in. (15.1 cm.).
Diameter of bowl, 4¾ in. (12.2 cm.).
Type: La Plata Black-on-red. Characteristic of Pueblo I-II.
UCM No. 9507.

Comments: SHEPARD: Anna O. Shepard, pottery specialist; long associated with the Carnegie Institution of Washington. MARTIN: Paul S. Martin of the Field Museum of Natural History; conducted much archaeological field work in the northern San Juan as well as in the Mogollon area to the south. In Pueblo I, the making of ladles from clay was still a relatively new departure and potters apparently felt no restriction in shaping them in any way that imagination might suggest. The most simple variety, an elongated scoop with upturned ends which presents no differentiation between bowl and handle, resembles a longitudinal section from the side of a gourd shell or a portion cut from the curve of a mountain sheep horn. A derivative of the half-gourd ladle is illustrated by this "jockey cap" shape, wherein the handle is shortened and broadened but not separated from the bowl so that it resembles the visor of the cap.

Ladles, or dippers as some prefer to call them, of the bowl-and-handle shape were made but are less numerous in Pueblo I than those based upon the gourd form. They usually have a hemispherical bowl from which protrude a wide variety of solid handles, oval to round in cross section.

Both types of ladles survived into Pueblo III in the San Juan, but the bowl-and-ladle style became the favored form and occurs in much greater frequency than the half-gourd type in later times.

Another jockey-cap ladle (UCM No. 9505) and three other half-gourd type ladles are shown in the lower part of Figure 9. Those pictured are:

UCM No.	Provenience	Type	Length
9505	Tohatchi Flats	Kana-a B/W	5 in. (12.7 cm.)
9533	Newcombe's Post	Escavada B/W (?)	5⅝ in. (14.3 cm.)
9308	Cottonwood Spgs.	Mancos B/W	6¾ in. (17.2 cm.)
9469	Tohatchi Flats	Red Mesa B/W	12 in. (30.6 cm.)

9617

Figure 10. San Juan, Pueblo I; pear-shaped olla.

PUEBLO I

LA PLATA, COLORADO-NEW MEXICO (FIGURE 10)

Very large, pear-shaped plain gray olla with horizontal loop handles at girdle. From Site 33, La Plata valley.

Dimensions: Height, 18 in. (45.6 cm.).
  Maximum diameter, 14 in. (35.6 cm.).
Type: Chapin Gray.
UCM No. 9618.

Comments: Large, full-bodied, narrow-necked ollas, or water or storage jars, were present in certain Basket Maker III dwellings, became more numerous in Pueblo I times, but declined rapidly and practically disappeared in Pueblo II. They were undecorated at first, but were both plain and decorated in later times. In discussing their presence in Pueblo I sites Morris (1939: 170) has noted that such containers occupied an important position in domestic economy. He felt they were used more for storage than for water, unless perhaps to store within the house water brought in smaller containers. Many of the great jars are of such size that when full would have constituted too heavy a load for the average bearer to have carried on her head, or slung in bag or net upon her back, up the steep trails from springs beneath the canyon ledges. When habitations and storerooms are excavated these vessels commonly are found crushed down upon the pottery clay, pottery temper, charred corn, beans, or grass seed which they once contained. Because of their size they were particularly subject to breakage during the collapse of walls and roof, and the surface area of each was sufficient to provide an astonishing bulk and quantity of sherds. It would appear that from one to several of these large containers constituted a necessary element of household equipment for every family in Pueblo I.

Two outstanding examples of large Pueblo I water or storage jars with decorated surfaces are shown in Figure 18.

The vessel shown in smaller scale is a less common shaped plain gray olla of Basket Maker III-Pueblo I times.

UCM No.	Provenience	Type	Height
9617	Near Farmington	Chapin Gray	14¼ in. (36.4 cm.)

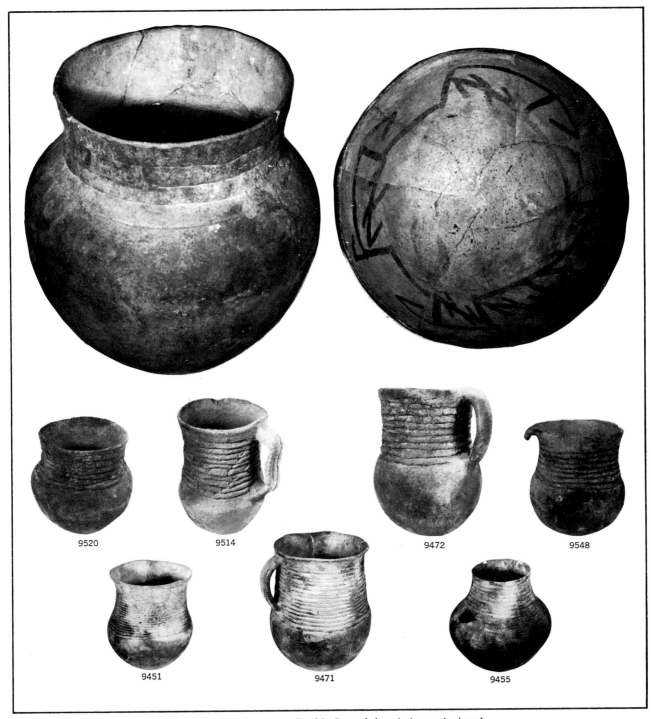

9520   9514   9472   9548

9451   9471   9455

Figure 11. San Juan, Pueblo I; neck-banded vessels, bowl.

Pueblo I

La Plata, Colorado-New Mexico (Figure 11)

(*Left.*) Banded-neck cook pot.

Dimensions: Height, 7⅛ in. (18.1 cm.).
Maximum diameter, 7 in. (17.8 cm.).
Type: Moccasin Gray.
UCM No. 9624.

Comments: Culinary jars with generally globular bodies and banded necks are the most diagnostic character of Pueblo I ceramics. Mouths of these vessels are almost always quite wide to make them suitable cooking utensils. The distinguishing and significant feature of this class of vessels was accomplished by leaving unobliterated the relatively broad concentric bands of clay from which the walls of the neck were built.

PUEBLO I

LA PLATA, COLORADO-NEW MEXICO (FIGURE 12)

(*Left.*) Small, very deep black-on-white bowl. Decoration consists of rows of large, brown-black dots sweeping down from rim-like radii to converge at center. Upper inch of body wall flares outward. The sudden flare and the steepness of the walls suggest that the vessel was built in a mold; and there is a 1½ inch impression that would appear to have been made by the rim coil of a basket, but it is too dim to be positively identified as such. This bowl is atypical for any period. It seems most probably to be Pueblo I. Found at the Holmes Group, La Plata valley, by P. T. Hudson.

Dimensions: Height, 3⅞ in. (10.1 cm.)
Maximum diameter, 6¼ in. (16.5 cm.).
Type: Mancos Black-on-white.
UCM No. 9373.

Comments: The HOLMES GROUP is a complex of archaeological remains in the La Plata valley named for the late W. H. Holmes, of the United States National Museum, who accompanied the Hayden Survey (1874-77) and first described these sites as well as other antiquities in southwestern Colorado.

(*Right.*) Black-on-white squash pot with vertically pierced lugs. Site 33, La Plata valley.

Dimensions: Height, 4⅜ in. (11.1 cm.).
Maximum diameter, 5⅜ in. (13.7cm.).
Mouth diameter, 3⅛ in. (8.1 cm.).
Type: Piedra Black-on-white.
UCM No. 9621.

Comments: Squash pots are defined as globular, depressed-spherical vessels with relatively wide orifice in the top. The term "seed jar" also is used for this style of vessel. The form likely was suggested by the use of containers fashioned of rinds of squash or gourds from which a disk surrounding the stem had been cut away. In most Basket Maker III localities the squash pot was perhaps the most common shape of cooking vessel and was most frequently undecorated. In the Pueblo I period, both decorated and plain squash pots appear not to have been used as culinary utensils. It was not a popular shape after Pueblo I, although it persisted in small numbers into Pueblo III.

Other squash pots in the Morris Collection, one (UCM No. 9436) with a strap handle, are shown in the lower half of Figure 12. Those pictured are:

UCM No.	Provenience	Type	Diameter
9436	La Plata valley	McElmo B/W	4¼ in. (11 cm.)
9628	Near Durango	Abajo R/O	8¾ in. (22.1 cm.)
9438	Near Gallup	Red Mesa B/W	10⅛ in. (25.7 cm.)
9488	Ackmen, Colorado	Mesa Verde B/W	8¾ in. (22.3 cm.)
9492	Near Kayenta	La Plata B/R (or Middleton B/R)	8½ in. (21.8 cm.)

(*Right.*) Black-on-white bowl.

Dimensions: Height, 3 in. (7.7 cm.).
Diameter at rim, 7¼ in. (18.3 cm.).
Type: La Plata Black-on-white, which is diagnostic of Basket Maker III and Pueblo I.
UCM No. 9623.

Both of these vessels came from a small dwelling between Buildings I and III, Site 33, La Plata district.

Comments: Additional examples of banded-neck vessels in the collection are shown in the bottom portion of Figure 11. Those pictured are:

UCM No.	Provenience	Type	Diameter
9520	Newcombe's Post	Mancos Gray	3½ in. (8.9 cm)
9514	Tohatchi Flats	Mancos Gray	4⅜ in. (11 cm.)
9472	Naschidi Post	Mancos Gray	5⅝ in. (14.4 cm.)
9548	Bennett's Peak	Mancos Gray	4⅝ in. (11.6 cm.)
9451	Red Rock Post	Mancos Gray	10½ in. (26.5 cm.)
9471	Tohatchi Flats	Mancos Gray	7 in. (17.8 cm.)
9455	Canyon de Chelly	Kana-a Gray	13⅞ in. (35.3 cm)

9436

9628

9438

9488

9492

FIGURE 12. San Juan, Pueblo I; bowl, squash pots or seed jars.

FIGURE 13. San Juan, Pueblo I; gourd-shaped vessels.

PUEBLO I

LA PLATA, COLORADO-NEW MEXICO (FIGURE 13)

Exceptionally fine black-on-white gourd-shaped vessel (illustrated in Morris, 1919, plate 72e). Found at Site 17, La Plata district, in 1914, when I was excavating for the University of Colorado Museum. I secured the specimen in exchange from the Museum many years later and had the missing portion of the handle restored by Mrs. Myer.

Dimensions: Height, 9⅝ in. (24.5 cm.).
Maximum diameter, 7 in. (17.9 cm.).
Type: Piedra Black-on-white.
UCM No. 9627.

Comments: MRS. MYER: Mrs. Alma F. Meyer, of Boulder, Colorado, frequently assisted Earl in repair and restoration of pottery. Gourd-shaped vessels, such as this example, obviously were modeled after some curve-necked member of the gourd family. They are confined almost exculsively to Pueblo I, and were made rarely in plain gray, most frequently in black-on-white, but not uncommonly in red ware.

Beneath the large view of the fine gourd-shaped vessel are examples of three other such vessels. Those pictured are:

UCM No.	Provenience	Type	Diameter
9476	Gallup-Shiprock road	Kana-a B/W	5 in. (12.8 cm.)
9541	Bennett's Peak	Piedra B/W	3⅝ in. (9.2 cm.)
9475	Gallup-Shiprock road	Kana-a B/W	6¼ in. (15.9 cm.)

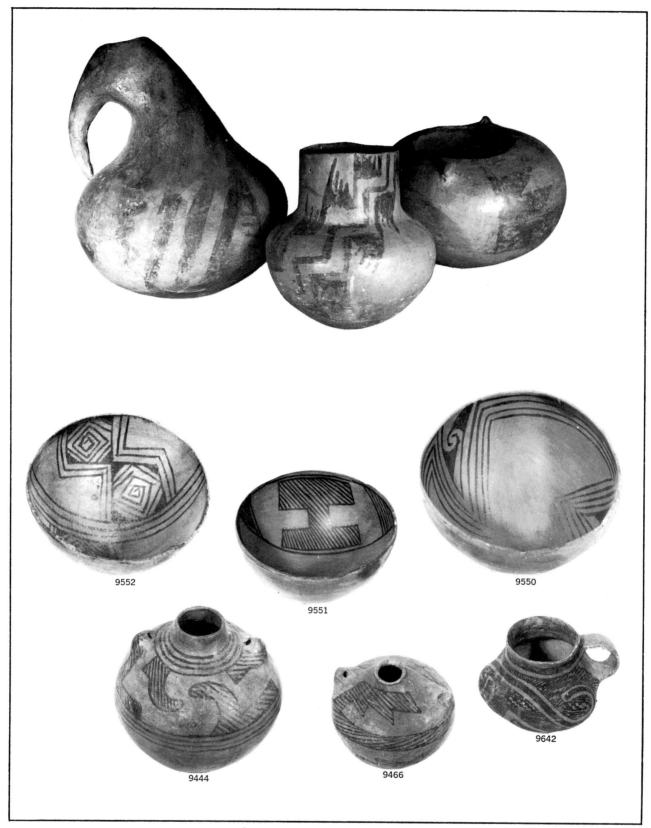

FIGURE 14. San Juan, Pueblo I; red wares in various shapes.

Pueblo I

La Plata, Colorado-New Mexico (Figure 14)

(*Left.*) Very large black-on-orange gourd-shaped vessel. From a small dwelling between Buildings I and III, Site 33, La Plata district.

Dimensions: Height, 9⅜ in. (23.8 cm.).
Diameter at bulbous portion, 8⅛ in. (20.6 cm.).
Type: Abajo Red-on-orange.
UCM No. 9620.

(*Middle.*) Small black-on-red vase. This is of terminal Basket Maker III or Pueblo I age. A Navajo brought this into Shiprock, New Mexico, and traded it to Bruce Barnard, and it was secured from him by Ann.

Dimensions: Height, 6 in. (15.2 cm.).
Maximum diameter, 5¾ in. (14.7 cm.).
Type: Abajo Red-on-orange.
UCM No. 9461.

Comments: The ANN referred to above was Ann Axtell Morris. Earl and Ann were married in 1923; she passed away in 1945.

(*Right.*) Very fine black-on-orange squash pot with pierced lugs. Found by Clint Wagner some miles west of the La Plata valley, about opposite Site 41. Purchased from him in 1934.

Dimensions: Height, 4¾ in. (12.2 cm.).
Maximum diameter, 7⅝ in. (19.2cm.).
Type: Abajo Red-on-orange.
UCM No. 9626.

Comments: Abajo Red-on-orange, considered a red ware although it is usually quite orange, and La Plata Black-on-red are locally manufactured types during Pueblo I-early Pueblo II times.

Additional San Juan area black-on-red vessels of the Pueblo I-Pueblo II periods are shown in the lower half of Figure 14. The bowls in the upper row are from the eastern San Juan, while those in the bottom row are more typical of the Kayenta region to the west. Those pictured are:

UCM No.	Provenience	Type	Diameter
9552	Bennett's Peak	La Plata B/R	8 in. (20.5 cm.)
9551	Bennett's Peak	La Plata B/R	8⅜ in. (21.5 cm.)
9550	Bennett's Peak	La Plata B/R	8⅝ in. (21.9 cm.)
9444	Red Rock Post	Tusayan B/R	7 in. (17.8 cm.)
9466	Fort Defiance	Tusayan B/R	5¾ in. (14.7 cm.)
9642	Apache County, Arizona	Tusayan B/R	5½ in. (13.9 cm.)

PUEBLO I

CANYON DE CHELLY, ARIZONA (FIGURE 15)

(*Left.*) Black-on-white bird-shaped vessel, Pueblo I age. Tail and wings in relief, a flat protuberance jutting forward from the breast. The handle is an adaptation from gourd shape—hollow, and tapering from a broad attachment at the back of the neck to touch, but not to join, the center of the back. From the knoll on the east side of the sand flat between Cozy McSparron's and the mouth of Canyon de Chelly.

Dimensions: Height, 3⅛ in. (8 cm.).
Length, 5⅞ in. (14.9 cm.).
Type: Black Mesa Black-on-white.
UCM No. 9456.

(*Right.*) Small black-on-white pitcher with handle that seems to represent a deer's foot turned upside down. Bought from a Navajo woman in Canyon de Chelly.

Dimensions: Height, 5 in. (12.6 cm.).
Maximum diameter, 4⅛ in. (10.4 cm.).
Type: Black Mesa Black-on-white.
UCM No. 9453.

FIGURE 15. San Juan, Pueblo I; globular-bodied pitchers, bird-shaped vessel.

Comments: Pitchers appeared in Basket Maker III as vessels with more or less globular bodies and relatively short, wide nearly straight necks which rise from the bodies without a sharp line of demarcation. The handles are a simple curve spanning from the rim, or slightly below it, to the incurve of the body wall. Most are plain surfaced. Pueblo I pitchers, of which this is an example, occur in plain gray, gray with banded neck, and black-on-white. Rarely they were manufactured in red ware. The shape gained rapidly in popularity during this period. Body forms range from squat, wide-mouthed to elongated pear-shaped, but the average is distinctly globular. Most of the necks taper toward the top and comprise about one-fourth of the altitude of the pitcher. Seldom is there a true line of separation between neck and body. Handles reach from the margin of the rim to a point on the body wall not far above the area of greatest diameter.

Eight other examples of globular-bodied pitchers are illustrated in the bottom part of Figure 15. They range in age from Basket Maker III to Pueblo II. Those pictured are:

UCM No.	Provenience	Type	Diameter
9511	Tohatchi Flats	Chapin Gray	5⅞ in. (14.9 cm.)
9561	La Plata valley	Chapin Gray	10 in. (25.4 cm.)
9486	Chaco Canyon	Kana-a B/W	5⅞ in. (15.1 cm.)
9477	Gallup-Shiprock road	Kana-a B/W	3½ in. (8.8 cm.)
9518	Newcombe's Post	Kana-a B/W	3⅜ in. (8.6 cm.)
9506	Tohatchi Flats	Kana-a B/W	3⅞ in. (9.9 cm.)
9474	Gallup-Shiprock road	Black Mesa B/W	5½ in. (14.2 cm.)
9440	Near Gallup	Red Mesa B/W	7½ in. (19.1 cm.)

Pueblo I

Navajo Reservation, New Mexico (Figure 16)

(*Left.*) Black-on-white bowl. Heavy coat of fugitive red paint on exterior.

Dimensions: Height, 3⅝ in. (9.3 cm.).
Maximum diameter, 8 in. (20.3 cm.).
Type: Piedra Black-on-white.
UCM No. 9504.

(*Right.*) Black-on-white canteen. Lug handles horizontally pierced.

Dimensions: Height, 6⅛ in. (15.7 cm.).
Maximum diameter, 5⅜ in. (13.8 cm.).
Type: Piedra Black-on-white.
UCM No. 9503.

In the summer of 1929 Ann and I came in from camp at Antelope House, Canyon del Muerto, to meet Dr. Wissler, his wife, and daughter at Gallup. There we had to lay over a day because of rains which made the clay road to Chinlee impassable. In order to kill the afternoon most painlessly, Ann and I drove out to the Tohatchi Flats, where I dug between showers. In an extensive but poorly defined refuse area just west of the road and about half way across the valley, I secured these vessels. The burial was that of a very large-boned adult male, lying on the left side of the back, with the head toward the southwest, flexed knees elevated and leaning against the wall of the pit. The bowl and canteen were nested by the left hip, so that the leg bones lay diagonally upward and across them.

Comments: DR. WISSLER: Clark Wissler, Curator of Anthropology, American Museum of Natural History, New York; now deceased. The American Museum of Natural History sponsored Earl's long range excavation program at Aztec Ruin, New Mexico, and a series of archaeological investigations in Canyon de Chelly and Canyon del Muerto, Arizona.

Lower section of Figure 16 shows the remainder of the canteen-shaped pots in the collection. Those pictured are:

UCM No.	Provenience	Type	Diameter
9519	Newcombe's Post	Kiatuthlana B/W	5 in. (12.7 cm.)
9325	Near Farmington	McElmo B/W	4⅞ in. (12.3 cm.)
9305	La Plata valley	Mesa Verde B/W	3½ in. (9.1 cm.)
9487	Reserve, New Mexico	Tularosa B/W	5⅛ in. (12.9 cm.)
9540	Bennett's Peak	Kana-a B/W	5⅜ in. (13.7 cm.)
9341	Blanding, Utah	Mancos B/W	8⅛ in. (20.7 cm.)

FIGURE 16. San Juan, Pueblo I; canteens, bowl.

9619   9622   9473

FIGURE 17. San Juan, Pueblo I; pitchers, bowl, jar.

Pueblo I

Navajo Reservation, New Mexico (Figure 17)

(*Left.*) Very large black-on-white pitcher.

Dimensions: Height, 9⅛ in. (23.1 cm.).
Maximum diameter, 7⅞ in. (20.2 cm.).
Type: Kana-a Black-on-white.
UCM No. 9537.

(*Right.*) Black-on-white pitcher. Animal effigy with hind feet attached to top of handle and front ones to rim of the vessel.

Dimensions: Height, 6⅜ in. (16.2 cm.).
Maximum diameter, 5½ in. (14 cm.).
Type: Kana-a Black-on-white.
UCM No. 9538.

There can be little doubt that these two pitchers are the work of the same potter. They are similar in shape and decoration, and identical in general effect. Moreover, they were found in burials from the same building.

One of the larger houses situated at about the center of the Bennett's Peak Group had two refuse heaps—a relatively huge one, oval in outline, with longer axis from east to west, paralleling the building to the south; and another, deep, but of smaller area, piled up against, and reaching westward from, the house. The larger pitcher was found in the large trash mound; the other in the refuse heap at the west, 1922.

Comments: Earl's intimate knowledge of a very large quantity of Southwestern pottery, frequently gained through his own excavations, led him to observe and describe groups of vessels that he believed to have been the work of individual potters. This is one such instance. Other examples of this phenomenon are discussed in his voluminous report upon archaeological remains in the La Plata district (Morris, 1939: 177-178).

Three other pieces of pottery illustrating characteristic Pueblo I decorative elements are shown below the two pitchers. Those pictured are:

UCM No.	Provenience	Type	Diameter
9619	La Plata valley	Piedra B/W	9¼ in. (23.4 cm.)
9622	La Plata valley	Piedra B/W	8¼ in. (21 cm.)
9473	Gallup-Shiprock road	Kana-a B/W	9⅝ in. (24.5 cm.)

PUEBLO I

NAVAJO RESERVATION, ARIZONA (FIGURE 18)

(*Left.*) Enormous black-on-white olla. Concave base. Loop handles set slightly below the girdle. A break of curve just above shoulder—sharp inward turn for a distance, from the upper margin of which the remainder of the body rises with steeper curve. Asymmetry of bottom shows that that portion was built inside a mold.

Dimensions: Height, 16¼ in. (41 cm.).
Maximum diameter, 14⅝ in. (37.2 cm.).
Type: Kana-a Black-on-white.
UCM No. 9449.

(*Right.*) Enormous black-on-white olla. Flattened bottom. Two-strand loop handles placed well below the girdle. A break of curve above the shoulder like that of the other olla in this illustration.

Dimensions: Height, 17⅛ in. (43.4 cm.).
Maximum diameter, 14½ in. (36.7 cm.).
Type: Kana-a Black-on-white.
UCM No. 9448.

In the arroyo-cut terrain northeast of an isolated mesa several miles north of the Red Rock Post there are some Navajo settlements and a good many traces of earlier aboriginal occupation. Not more than half a mile toward the Lukachukai Mountain from the isolated mesa there are the dim remains of a building the walls of which were stone in their basal course, but from the dearth of rocks lying about, must have been of some other material thence upward. What remains of the structure is at the very western edge of a deep arroyo. I scratched about a bit in this spot during the Bernheimer Expedition of 1930, but, finding that the structure had been burned and that only a few inches of earth covered the old floors, judged there was little purpose in going further. It was at this ruin, in the very edge of the area that I had previously turned, where four vessels including these two large ollas were found.

In June of 1932, when I was en route with Willard Fraser from Boulder, Colorado to Chinlee, Arizona to join Albright, then Director of the National Park Service, for an inspection of Canyon de Chelly National Monument, I stopped for gas at the Red Rock Post. While I was chatting with Stolworthy, the proprietor, Willard went over to the old mission hospital building about 200 yards northeast of the spot in search of Eugene Topahastso. Eugene had been my interpreter all the summer of 1931, while we were working in the Prayer Rock caves, and the last we knew of him he had taken employment from the missionary—

Luke, I believe his name was—stationed at Red Rock. As I came out of the store Willard shouted to me to come over. I crossed the low ground between the buildings, started up the flight of stairs that led to the high porch, and when my eyes came above the level of the latter, my mouth fell open in astonishment, for there were the four vessels sitting in plain view. Never in my life had I seen ollas of the size and quality of the two large ones, nor have I had that experience since. I asked Eugene to tell me exactly where he had found them, and he described the site so minutely that I had no trouble in recognizing it.

The vessels were in a slab-lined, slab-covered storage recess beneath the floor of one of the rooms of the ruin. Having been protected by the slab cover, they were unbroken and undamaged by the fire that had once raged above them. However, before the cutting of the adjacent arroyo, the site of the ruin had long been damp and carbon deposited in the porous vessel walls by the water they absorbed had stained much of the surfaces that should have been almost shell-white from light brown to almost black. I regard these vessels as transitional between Pueblo I and II.

A number of people had tried to purchase the specimens from Eugene, but he had decided to hold them for me. I greatly appreciated his loyalty in doing so. My offer for the group (4) was twenty-five dollars, which he accepted and seemed to be entirely satisfied.

Comments: BERNHEIMER EXPEDITION: Charles L. Bernheimer, wealthy cottonbroker and patron of the American Museum of Natural History, for over a decade beginning in 1920 made fourteen pack trips through remote districts of the Four Corners. Earl became Bernheimer's guest for five trips (1921, '22, '23, '29, and '30) which were known as the Bernheimer Expeditions under the auspices of the American Museum of Natural History. Earl accomplished a considerable amount of archaeological exploration on these trips.
WILLARD FRASER: Participated in several of Morris' expeditions. Now mayor of Billings, Montana.
ALBRIGHT: Horace M. Albright, Director of the National Park Service, 1929 to 1933.
Pueblo I pottery decoration, as demonstrated by specimens in this collection, was still in its formative stage and hence markedly fluid and variable. Certain trends may be recognized but these had not become sufficiently crystallized to lead the pot painters into any definite or restricted tradition. Many styles of vessel treatment could be regarded as the work of individual potters rather than as patterns binding on the whole contemporary art.

A rather small number of decorative elements were used by pottery painters of Pueblo I. They may be listed as follows: the plain straight line, more often narrow than wide; the straight line, fringed or "ticked" on one side or crossbarred; the squiggly line, sometimes made by drawing a wavy one over an original straight line. The triangle occurs, outlined merely, or solid. The solid ones may be fringed. The solid terrace is present, both fringed and plain. The line-bordered, dot-filled space is frequently employed. True curvilinear patterns are conspicuous by their absence. Naturalistic representations are occasionally to be encountered. The majority of Pueblo I black-on-white decorations give the effect of being "light" rather than "heavy" due to the preponderance of narrow lines (Morris, 1939: 179).
Black-on-red ware, which made its appearance late in Basket Maker III, reached its highest prevalence in Pueblo I. Structurally it was very well perfected, and when one considers that the rest of the ceramic complex was in a formative process, foreign origin is suspected but it has not been proven.

FIGURE 18. San Juan, Pueblo I; large ollas.

Pueblo II

San Juan Valley, New Mexico (Figure 19)

(*Left rear.*) Small hachured Chaco pitcher. Found in 1923 in refuse heap burials at a small ruin which has since been completely leveled down. It was situated in the slowly rising flat that slopes south from the San Juan, about one-half mile west of the Shiprock bridge.

Dimensions: Height, 5½ in. (14 cm.).
Maximum diameter, 4¼ in. (10.8 cm.).
Neck height, 2⅝ in. (6 cm.).
Type: Chaco Black-on-white, more characteristic of Pueblo III.
UCM No. 9460.

Comments: Pitchers were relatively plentiful in Pueblo II. Basically resembling those of Pueblo I, they do exhibit an incipient line of demarcation between neck and body, and the necks are straight or only slightly tapering.

(*Middle rear.*) Small canteen. Eyelet handles slightly above girdle.

Dimensions: Height 5¼ in. (13.4 cm.).
Maximum diameter, 5⅞ in. (14.8 cm.).
Type: Gallup Black-on-white.
UCM No. 9457.

(*Left middle.*) Medium sized black-on-white bowl. This and the canteen listed above are from the San Juan valley, just south of the highway, about 5 miles east of Shiprock.

Dimensions: Height, 3½ in. (8.9 cm.).
Maximum diameter, 8¼ in. (21.1 cm.).
Type: Mancos Black-on-white.
UCM No. 9458.

In 1921 I drove Fred Hinchman and his mother and father from Aztec to Shiprock to visit Mrs. Axtell, Ann, and her brother, whom they had met on the train coming over Cumbres Pass. Thus began my acquaintance with the Axtells, who were staying with Mrs. Barnard and her son Bruce, the trader. Ann was much interested in the ruins of the vicinity; hence it was agreed that I should come down some time later for a digging expedition. Shortly afterward Ann found out from the Navajo, through Bruce Barnard, that there was a large sandstone ruin on the south bluff of the San Juan, approximately 6 miles upstream from Shiprock. When I did come down, she, Bruce Barnard, and Lane took me to the spot. We managed to get the old Ford down to the north bank of the stream, then waded across to the ruin. It turned out to be a good-sized Chaco pueblo built of sandstone. It was clear from the potsherds scattered about that it, in common with the rest of the pueblos along the San Juan, had been reoccupied by a Mesa Verde group. Whatever refuse piles there may have been had been removed by erosion, and I saw no chance of finding any specimens without more excavation than could be done in a single day. Hence I suggested a return to the north side of the river to a place that I had noticed in my trips up and down the valley and had intended to investigate. At this point the large canal that irrigates the north side of the valley had been cut deep through the area just south of a small cobblestone ruin. Although earth removed from the cut obscured the original surface, I knew that the path of the canal lay where the trash pile should have been, and thought there might be something exposed in the bank. Ann's first remark when she saw my choice of a location was, "Well, what a place to dig in."

Under the yard or more of freshly turned earth the dark stratum of the refuse heap was plainly discernable. I began working along the face on the north side, rolling far more earth down into the canal than the maintenance crew would have approved of. After only a few minutes work I found the burial of a child and gave Ann a trowel with which to uncover it. There remained only the disintegrated bones—no pottery whatever. Then, a few feet farther to the west I struck the edge of a slab covering the burial of an adult. As Ann worked toward the head of this grave and came upon the bowl and canteen, she withdrew her criticism as to the choice of the site. Naturally enough, the vessels were hers, and they remained in the Axtell home in Omaha until some years after our marriage.

FIGURE 19. San Juan, Pueblo II; bowls, pitcher, canteen, bird-shaped vessel.

(*Right rear.*) Large bowl with peaked bottom and widely flaring walls. A single lug-like handle on one side about an inch below the rim. All-over hachured pattern. Found at same site as pitcher in left rear of illustration.

Dimensions: Height, 4½ in. (11.4 cm.).
Maximum diameter, 11 in. (27.7 cm.).
Type: Dogoszhi Black-on-white. Pueblo II-III.
UCM No. 9459.

(*Front middle.*) Black-on-white bird-form vessel. Found by Earl Morris near the Eldredge Mission on the south side of the San Juan, southwest of Farmington, during Christmas vacation, 1908. This was in the trash pile burial of an adult, accompanied by a large bowl with black and white interior pattern and corrugated exterior, dating from early Pueblo III. The bird-form vessel, of crude workmanship and shaped more like a flatiron than anything else, has a round hole nearly one-half inch in diameter, of intentional origin, in one side of the bottom.

Dimensions: Height, 4⅝ in. (11.8 cm.).
Length, 7⅜ in. (18.9 cm.).
Maximum width, 4⅞ in. (12.4 cm.).
Type: McElmo Black-on-white.
UCM No. 9335.

9374

9450

9375

9534

9464

Figure 20. San Juan, Pueblo II; bowls, olla.

PUEBLO II

LOWER ANIMAS VALLEY, NEW MEXICO (FIGURE 20)

(*Left.*) Very large flat-bottomed, steep-walled black-on-white bowl. Horizontal loop handles on opposite sides about an inch below the rim. Corrugated exterior, somewhat wiped down. All-over hachured pattern. Two opposing quadrants consisting of straight-lined hachure, while the hachure of the other pair is "squiggled." In the winter of 1930-31, P. T. Hudson of Aztec gave me a quantity of fragments that obviously belonged to one black-on-white olla. I set them up and found that they composed practically all of the vessel but the handles and the neck. Upon inquiry Hudson said that he had found the fragments on the floor of a room in a cobblestone ruin on the rim of the mesa just west of the deep draw which emerges from the second terrace, north of the Aztec Ruin, immediately back of the Abrams ranch buildings. With the hope of finding the missing fragments, I got him to show me the spot, and dug over the remainder of the room. He had only trenched along the walls. The desired fragments of the olla were found in a prairie dog hole beneath the floor. Crushed down and scattered over an area about a yard across, practically at the center of the chamber, were the fragments of the bowl here listed.

Dimensions: Height, 6⅛ in. (15.5 cm.).
Maximum diameter, 12¼ in. (31 cm.).
Type: Mancos Black-on-white.
UCM No. 9348.

Comments: In Pueblo II and early Pueblo III there was a slight crossing of the techniques of corrugating and painting, resulting in bowls with corrugated exteriors and painted interiors.

LA PLATA VALLEY, NEW MEXICO (FIGURE 20)

(*Right.*) Medium sized bowl with all-over black-on-white pattern. Found by P. T. Hudson at the Holmes Group, La Plata valley, New Mexico.

Dimensions: Height, 3¼ in. (8.2 cm.).
Maximum diameter, 8¼ in. (21 cm.).
Type: Cortez Black-on-white.
UCM No. 9376.

Comments: Among the decorative elements employed during Pueblo II, the straight line, more often narrow but sometimes broad, is probably the most basic. Fringed and crossbarred lines occur, but rarely. The squiggled line is extremely prevalent, almost always relatively narrow and delicate. Short squiggled lines drawn diagonally or straight across bands bounded by straight lines constitute the wavy hachure which in point of origin is earlier than straight-line crosshatching. Checkerboarding with either rectangular or triangular units is fairly common. The terrace and the triangle in simple form do occur, but more frequently they are fringed or dotted along one or more sides. These figures also often bear a curved or spiral line extension from their tips. Bands prevail that are composed of curve-tipped terraces or triangles emanating alternatively from the opposite borders, their tips interlocking (Morris, 1939: 192). Locally made black-on-red was extremely scarce during Pueblo II and III.

Five other vessels in the collection, exhibiting characteristic design elements of Pueblo II age, are shown in the lower half of Figure 20. Those pictured are:

UCM No.	Provenience	Type	Diameter
9374	Holmes Group	Cortez B/W	11⅝ in. (29.4 cm.)
9450	Red Rock Post	Kana-a B/W	9½ in. (24 cm.)
9375	Holmes Group	Cortez B/W	8⅞ in. (22.6 cm.)
9534	Bennett's Peak	Sosi B/W	7¾ in. (19.7 cm.)
9464	Newcombe's Post	Black Mesa B/W	8⅞ in. (22.6 cm.)

9513

FIGURE 21. San Juan, Pueblo II; ollas, seed jar, bowl.

PUEBLO II

NAVAJO RESERVATION, ARIZONA-NEW MEXICO
(FIGURE 21)

(*Left.*) Black-on-red seed jar. Heavily fire-clouded, with tiny knob-like lugs on opposite sides about an inch and a half from the rim. Looked at from above, these lugs would appear to be vertically pierced, as is customary for vessels of the period. However, the tiny holes passed not downward through the lug, but inward, through the vessel wall. These holes were punched through from the outside while the clay was green. Found by an Indian 6 miles west of the Bennett's Peak group, 1933.

Dimensions: Height, 4⅛ in. (10.6 cm.).
Maximum diameter, 6½ in. (16.5 cm.).
Type: Abajo Red-on-orange. Characteristic of Pueblo I.
UCM No. 9554.

(*Middle.*) Large corrugated jar of the tall, bell-mouthed variety. A superlative specimen. The narrow coil maintains a surprisingly uniform width, and the deep indenting strokes were so carefully spaced and controlled that there is a pattern with ribs diagonally ascending in both directions as if a meshwork had been superimposed upon the basic coils.

There is a large group of ruins dating all the way from Basket Maker III to the Mesa Verde occupation (Pueblo III) of the district, situated some 5 or 6 miles northwest of the Newcombe Post at Nava and perhaps 7 miles southwest of the Bennett's Peak group. White men have no name for the broad valley, and I did not learn what the Navajo call it. I did considerable digging in the refuse areas of several of the ruins for the American Museum of Natural History in December, 1922. In 1929 I returned to the site to find that nearly all of it that I had not dug had been completely overturned by relic hunters. I worked over one room in a small ruin near the east end of the group. The above vessel had been buried as a cache pot beneath the floor.

Dimensions: Height, 12½ in. (31.9 cm.).
Maximum diameter, 10⅞ in. (27.6 cm.).
Type: Mancos Corrugated.
UCM No. 9532.

Comments: The development of culinary ware witnessed by Pueblo II consisted of progression from concentric banding of vessel necks through narrow, parallel concentric ridging to the true spiral corrugation; and of the spread of corrugated surface ornamentation to include the entire exterior of the vessel (Morris, 1939: 186). Corrugations were created by leaving visible on the surface of the vessel the construction coils and the indentations made with the thumb as the coils were pinched together. Jars normally were greater in height than in diameter, had only slightly flaring rims, and their mouths were almost as wide as the widest diameter of the pot.

(*Right.*) Medium sized black-on-white bowl. Heavy-line curvilinear band pattern. Finely corrugated exterior. Found in 1928 in the Red Rocks district, Arizona, associated with an adult skeleton which was eroding from near a ruin consisting of a long string of rooms, apparently only one tier in width, running from east to west. The skeleton lay on its back, with knees elevated, head to the north. At the right of the skull was this vessel and one other. I am not able to place the vessel exactly as to type. I believe it is of western origin or influence.

Dimensions: Height, 3⅝ in. (9.1 cm.).
Maximum diameter, 7¼ in. (18.4 cm.).
Type: Black Mesa Black-on-white.
UCM No. 9445.

Comments: The corrugated jar inset in the lower part of Figure 21 is another example of the bell-mouthed variety most characteristic of Pueblo II. It may be described as follows:

UCM No.	Provenience	Type	Diameter
9513	Tohatchi Flats	Mancos Corrugated	5¾ in. (14.7 cm.)

FIGURE 22. San Juan, Pueblo II; effigy vessel, bowl, bowl-and-handle dipper.

Pueblo II

NAVAJO RESERVATION, NEW MEXICO (FIGURE 22)

(*Top.*) Black-on-white ring-bottomed effigy pitcher. The body is doughnut-shaped, hollow ring. On one side it swings forward to represent the breast of a bird. Above this swelling rises the thick neck, surmounted by a relatively huge head, from the top of which emerges the mouth of the vessel. A three-strand, vertical loop handle swings from the junction of neck and ring to the top of the back of the head. This was found in the summer of 1925, during the time that Ann, Oscar Tatman, and I were living in the abandoned hogan at Bennett's Peak, finding shelter under the dwindling portion of it as we gradually stripped the covering timbers from the door westward for fuel.

Dimensions: Height, 5½ in. (14.1 cm.).
Maximum diameter, 5⅜ in. (13.8 cm.).
Type: Kana-a Black-on-white, or Black Mesa Black-on-white.
UCM No. 9539.

(*Bottom.*) Black-on-white bowl. Drawing of a human footprint at center of bottom. A wide heavy-line pattern on exterior. It would appear that the exterior pattern was done in the white clay used as a slip on the interior. Pattern seems to have been drawn with two fingertips freely dipped in a thick mixture. First, two wavering fingerwidth lines were drawn directly across from rim to rim, about an inch apart. Then from these, at right angles, comparably broad irregular stripes were drawn to the rim, seven on one side and six on the other. I have observed no other example of such treatment. In the summer of 1925 I spent an afternoon and part of the following forenoon along the two and one-half miles of Captain Tom's Wash west from Newcombe's Post. In this distance ruins of all ages from Pueblo I through early Pueblo III are numerous, many of them badly washed and windcut. With almost no digging at all, I secured this vessel and five others.

Dimensions: Height, 3¼ in. (8.2 cm.).
Maximum diameter, 7⅛ in. (18.3 cm.).
Type: Mancos Black-on-white.
UCM No. 9524.

Comments: The fragmentary dipper depicted to the right of the bowl has another design associated with the feet—a pair of notched-toe sandals. It may be described as follows:

UCM No.	Provenience	Type	Diameter
9493	Near Gallup	Mancos B/W (?)	5⅛ in. (13.1 cm.)

PUEBLO II

NAVAJO RESERVATION, NEW MEXICO (FIGURE 23)

(*Left.*) Large black-on-red bowl. Hard thin ware, extremely smooth inside and out, with shadowy black pattern lustrous in the proper light. From the Bennett's Peak group near the Gallup-Shiprock road. This group of ruins had never been touched by the shovel previous to work that I did there for the American Museum in the summer of 1920. As is so often the case, it needs but a beginning at a certain spot to bring relic hunters to it like buzzards from far and near. The rapidity with which the trash mounds were being turned upside down led me to pause more often at Bennett's Peak than anywhere else along the line when I saw an opportunity to dig, even if only for a few hours. It was another case of feeling no guilt in securing all the specimens that I could before they became scattered far and wide and all record of them lost.

Dimensions: Height, 4⅝ in. (11.8 cm.).
Maximum diameter, 10 in. (25.5 cm.).
Type: La Plata Black-on-red.
UCM No. 9549.

(*Right.*) Black-on-white pitcher. A vertical loop handle, circular in cross section, swings from slightly below the rim down to the junction of the body wall and neck. From a like distance below the rim and about an inch on either side of the handle, two poorly modeled arms wing out, so that the hand of the left clasps the handle at center, and that of the right grasps it a little higher up. This effigy pitcher was found along Captain Tom's Wash west of Newcombe's Post in 1921 in a crack in a ledge cropping at a considerable distance from any ruin then visible. I noticed a sandstone slab of different color and quality from that of the ledge, lying horizontally where it had been exposed by the wind. It was above the skeleton of an adult wedged down into a fissure. The effigy pitcher was the only vessel that had been buried with it.

Dimensions: Height, 6⅞ in. (17.6 cm.).
Maximum diameter, 5¼ in. (13.4 cm.).
Type: Kana-a Black-on-white.
UCM No. 9525.

Comments: This effigy likely represents Kokopelli, the Humpbacked Flute Player. The pitcher handle may be interpreted as a flute, and the hands rest on it in playing position. Each hand has five fingers. Kokopelli is a Hopi deity said to be influential in hunting, producing rain, and as a source of fertile crops and human fecundity. He is also represented in the pantheons of several New Mexico pueblos. In addition to playing a flute he is always shown to be humpbacked. Depictions of this personage in prehistoric Anasazi pictographs and petroglyphs and in designs drawn upon pottery vessels indicate the concept to be one of ancient origin in the Southwest. A somewhat similar Kokopelli effigy vessel, discovered in a ruin to the southeast of Chaco Canyon and said to date from early Pueblo III times, has been described by Marjorie Lambert (1966: 21-25).

The lower part of Figure 23 shows an enlargement of the handle and arms of the effigy pot, and a painted depiction of Kokopelli in the bottom of a dipper bowl. The dipper bowl is described as follows:

UCM No.	Provenience	Type	Diameter
9494	Near Gallup	Tularosa B/W	5⅜ in. (13.7 cm.)

FIGURE 23. San Juan, Pueblo II; bowl, Kokopelli effigy pitcher, dipper bowl with Kokopelli design.

FIGURE 24. San Juan, Pueblo II; unusual bowls, submarine-shaped vessels.

PUEBLO II

NAVAJO RESERVATION, NEW MEXICO (FIGURE 24)

(*Upper left.*) Black-on-white vessel. Consists of three small bowls joined together, with a flat strap handle bifurcated at the end, jutting out from the junction of two of them, so that the shape, when viewed from above, might be likened to that of a three-leaf clover. Pueblo II or early Pueblo III.

Dimensions: Height, 1¼ in. (3.2 cm.).
Length, 7⅜ in. (18.8 cm.).
Type: Black Mesa Black-on-white (?).
UCM No. 9542.

Comments: This and the small gray vessel described below are not common shapes, but illustrate the variety that individual potters sometimes introduced into their products during the Pueblo II period.

(*Upper right.*) Dark gray vessel. This unslipped, undecorated vessel is composed of two tiny bowls joined together by an inch-long bar hollowed out at the top to form a minute bowl-like container.

Dimensions: Height, 1⅛ in. (2.7 cm.).
Length, 3⅝ in. (9.3 cm.).
Type: Lino Gray or Chapin Gray.
UCM No. 9543.

These two vessels were associated with a burial in a ruin in the Bennett's Peak group, 1929.

LOWER ANIMAS VALLEY, NEW MEXICO (FIGURE 24)

(*Lower left.*) Small Mesa Verde submarine-shaped vessel (illustrated in Morris, 1939: Pl. 302n). From a subfloor burial in the cobblestone ruin which is located south of the Prewitt pasture cut-off between Aztec and the La Plata, and just east of the lane that runs from north to south through the Holmes Group.

Dimensions: Height, 2⅜ in. (6 cm.).
Length, 5½ in. (13.9 cm.).
Type: Mesa Verde Black-on-white.
UCM No. 9435.

(*Lower right.*) Black-on-white submarine-shaped vessel of early Pueblo III age. "Doorknob" handles in line of longer axis, one on each side of neck. Bold, black pattern, unlike, on opposite sides. Found on the Blake ranch, winter of 1903-'04, by William Buck, who had done a great amount of pothunting in Arizona and had worked in Chaco Canyon for the Hyde expeditions. He was married to the half-breed daughter of Salmon, who owned the land on the San Juan where the Salmon Ruin is located.

Dimensions: Height, 3½ in. (9.1 cm.).
Length, 7⅝ in. (19.3 cm.).
Type: Mancos Black-on-white or Escavada Black-on-white.
UCM No. 9329.

Comments: The submarine-shaped form originated in Basket Maker III and although seldom used, was not discarded until early Pueblo III. When handled, they typically are of the doorknob variety, although small transverse eyelets sometimes were employed. Pots of this shape could have served as canteens.

HYDE EXPEDITION: The Hyde expedition for explorations in the Southwest was conducted at Pueblo Bonito, Chaco Canyon, by the American Museum of Natural History between 1896 and 1899. It was named for Messrs. B. Talbot B. Hyde and Frederick E. Hyde, Jr., who financed the project.

FIGURE 25. San Juan, Pueblo III; effigy vessels.

PUEBLO III

SAN JUAN VALLEY, NEW MEXICO (FIGURE 25)

(*Top left.*) Effigy vessel, perhaps representative of deer or elk form (illustrated in Morris, 1939: plate 294 g-g'''). From Holmes Group, New Mexico, 1932.

Dimensions: Height, 5⅜ in. (13.7 cm.).
　　　　　　Width, 6 in. (15.2 cm.).
Type: Gallup Black-on-white (?).
UCM No. 9381.

(*Top right.*) Early Pueblo III effigy pitcher (illustrated in Morris, 1939: plate 294 e-e'). The base of the pitcher is an extremely well-modeled representation of a toad, with eyes, legs, and a rudiment of a tail in relief. Mouth and nostrils are cut in. From the middle of the back rises the tall, tapering neck. Handle restored. From Holmes Group.

Dimensions: Height, 5⅝ in. (14.3 cm.).
　　　　　　Length, 5¼ in. (13.4 cm.).
Type: Mesa Verde Black-on-white.
UCM No. 9380.

The deer or elk effigy, illustrated on the top left, and the toad effigy are the only complete effigy vessels that I know to have been found in the lower La Plata valley near the San Juan. They were found within 100 feet of each other in a refuse area on the eastern side of the Holmes Group, well toward the southern end of the mesa.

The deer effigy was unearthed by Arthur Stone. He and Hudson and, I think, one or two others drove over from Aztec for a Sunday's pothunting in the winter of 1932. Stone had opened up a pit no larger than a bushel basket when he came across this extraordinary specimen, and fortunately did not break it with the shovel. I first saw it on display at the Aztec Ruin in the summer of 1933. Stone was reported to be in Silverton. I went there to find him and was informed that the road crew with which he was working had moved to Gunnison. I trailed him there and found him about six-thirty in the morning cooking a panful of trout in a room above one of the stores on Main Street. I asked his price for the specimen, but he did not want to dispose of it. However, he was willing that I should borrow it for photography and description. Some time later he wrote me that I could have it at whatever price I thought fair. I sent him a check for $35.00.

The toad effigy was found by P. T. Hudson in the winter of 1933-34. Many times he had told me that if ever he found an effigy vessel he would make me a present of it, and he kept his word. There must have been one potter in the Holmes Group who specialized in effigies, for among the sherds on the extensive refuse area in which these two were found, and around the house mound whence this refuse evidently came, fragments of legs and heads of effigies have been picked up in considerable numbers.

Comments: Effigy vessels were never plentiful in the San Juan country, but apparently reached their peak of manufacture in early Pueblo III. These are outstanding examples of a type of vessel rarely recovered in whole or restorable condition.

(*Bottom.*) Black-on-white animal effigy, skunk-like head and black spots suggest that it may have been intended to represent a civet cat (illustrated in Morris, 1939: plate 294 f-f'). It is considerably battered. The right rear leg missing, the other three broken off, presumably at about half their original length, with the stubs ground smooth. Tail and ears are knocked off, the bail-like handle gone—all but a stub at either end—and the neck less than its original height, the irregular edge somewhat smoothed by rubbing.

This specimen was found by William Morris (no relative) in the spring of 1905 about 3 miles north of Farmington. He was riding down the Farmington Glade on a load of wood, and, at a point where on the east side of the valley the road swung close against the cliff, he saw the vessel on a level with his eye, lying in a barrel-sized cavity in the rock. It was, as far as I know, the first effigy vessel anywhere near complete that had been found in the vicinity of Farmington. I gave him no rest until I finally traded him out of it, giving him two dollars and a half and a box of shotgun shells in exchange.

Dimensions: Height, 3⅜ in. (8.8 cm.).
　　　　　　Length, 11⅛ in. (28.2 cm.).
Type: Mesa Verde Black-on-white.
UCM No. 9331.

PUEBLO III

SAN JUAN VALLEY, NEW MEXICO (FIGURE 26)

(*Left rear.*) Straight-sided Chaco pitcher. Found by Scott N. Morris in the winter of 1903 and '04 at the southern edge of the house on the Blake ranch, Farmington, New Mexico.

Dimensions: Height, 5⅝ in. (14.2 cm.).
Maximum diameter, 4⅜ in. (11.2 cm.).
Type: Chaco shape, but has carbon paint more like Mesa Verde; possibly McElmo Black-on-white.
UCM No. 9319.

(*Middle rear.*) Hachured Chaco pitcher. This is, I think, the most gracefully shaped pitcher that I have ever seen from the Southwest. The neck is unusually long, with a slight taper. The handle follows the slope of the neck and swings from slightly below the rim to a lower attachment at the girdle of the body. This point of attachment is one of the major features to account for the effect of the vessel—handles usually are attached to the neck somewhat above the shoulder. Said to have been found at one of the several ruins in the mouth of Huntington Canyon, which comes into the San Juan from the south a little way east of Farmington. It was brought in by one of the boys of the Head family and sold to Brah Me, who then had a curio store in Farmington. The boy said he picked it up at the mouth of a badger hole. I purchased it from Brah Me in 1915 for ten dollars.

Dimensions: Height, 8¾ in. (19.8 cm.).
Maximum diameter, 4¾ in. (12.3 cm.).
Type: Gallup Black-on-white.
UCM No. 9340.

(*Right rear.*) Tall straight-necked Chaco pitcher. Found by Scott N. Morris, lower La Plata valley, spring of 1904.

Dimensions: Height, 8½ in. (21.5 cm.).
Maximum diameter, 5¼ in. (13.4 cm.).
Type: Appears to be Chaco Black-on-white, but the heavy-lined design on the body is unusual.
UCM No. 9327.

(*Left front.*) Small bird-shaped pitcher. Along the lower few miles of the La Plata valley there are many small cobblestone ruins, most of them of Mesa Verde age. They seem to have been briefly occupied, and although they have been pretty thoroughly rummaged, they have yielded very few specimens. One day in 1934 Gustav Stromsvik and Willard Fraser and I spent a few hours at one which is situated 2 or 3 miles from the mouth of the river, on the east side of the valley. The structure there had consisted of a single row of four rooms running east and west, with a fifth jutting southward from the easternmost. The sub-floor burial of an adult in the northeast corner of the latter yielded some vessels. This early Pueblo III pitcher was under a slab beneath the western room of the struc- ture. Being so much older than the other vessels, it is most reasonable to suppose that the infant with which it had been put away was buried in the open before the Mesa Verde dwelling chanced to be built above the spot.

Dimensions: Height, 3⅝ in. (9.3 cm.).
Length, 4⅛ in. (10.4 cm.).
Type: Mancos Black-on-white, more characteristic of Pueblo II.
UCM No. 9420.

Comments: GUSTAV STROMSVIK worked with Morris for many seasons in the Southwest and in Yucatan. He was valued by Earl for being a Jack-of-all-trades, a field archaeol- ogist, a mechanic, and an engineer.

9515

9407

9480

9337

9340

9434

9439

9336

FIGURE 26. San Juan, Pueblo III; pitchers, mugs, bird-shaped vessel.

(*Left front, middle.*) Large Mesa Verde mug. In 1927 while en route from Aztec to the La Plata valley to begin excavations with Shapiro in the Basket Maker III sites around the mouth of Long Hollow, I stopped on the crest of the north end of the Holmes Group to wait for the cars to catch up. To pass the time, I began looking for arrow points and before long saw a human bone in the edge of a recently dug pit in a small trash mound. The mug was by the face of the adult skeleton to which the bone belonged.

Dimensions: Height, 4⅝ in. (11.9 cm.).
Maximum diameter, 4⅝ in. (11.9 cm.).
Type: Mesa Verde Black-on-white.
UCM No. 9424.

Comments: SHAPIRO: Harry L. Shapiro, presently head curator of anthropology, American Museum of Natural History.

(*Right front, middle.*) Mesa Verde mug with lizard effigy on the handle. The mug impresses me as a very late Mesa Verde. The decoration is altogether typical in its layout, but was poorly conceived and carelessly applied. The handle is crooked and was flattened in against the vessel wall until there is no room for the fingers to reach beneath it. In distinct contrast is the workmanship on the lizard, which is, I think, the finest piece of Mesa Verde modeling that I have ever seen. The body lies flat against the handle, with the effect of bas-relief. From the undercutting evident along the sides of all features and the fact that the forward legs do not touch the handle as they join the body, there can be little doubt that the lizard was modeled separately, then appliqued to the handle.

This mug was found by G. C. Bero, of Farmington, near the Eldredge Mission, on the south side of the San Juan, 2 to 2½ miles southwest of Farmington, about 1905. There were several cobblestone ruins in this locality. They have long since been undermined and washed away by the river, which took a tremendous swing towards the south, principally during the great flood of 1911. To judge from what I saw on one visit to the locality and from other pottery which Mr. Bero found, the history of the group was typical of that of the Animas valley as a whole—Chaco in the first place, with Mesa Verde reoccupation.

Several times as the years passed I tried to secure the mug from Mr. Bero, but he did not want to part with it. After his death, it was purchased from the estate through the kind offices of Mrs. H. B. Sammons, who sent it to me early in November, 1942.

Dimensions: Height, 3⅛ in. (8.1 cm.).
Maximum diameter, 3⅝ in. (9.1 cm.).
Type: Mesa Verde Black-on-white.
UCM No. 9657.

(*Right front.*) Mesa Verde mug with keyhole opening in handle (illustrated in Morris, 1939, plate 303c). This vessel, along with seven others, was found under the following circumstances. During the winter of 1930-31 I found it necessary now and then to get away from Aztec for a brief change of scene. As might be expected, my first choice in the way of diversion was to go dig somewhere. Since everyone else who cared to was pothunting along the La Plata, my conscience did not disturb me for unearthing what I might before someone else got to it.

Near the south end of Site 41, not far from the foot of the mesa which borders the western side of it, there was a small house mound, little disturbed by previous digging, that I did not have time nor funds to open during the formal excavations of the summer of 1930. All told I worked for five days in this mound. The house had been of unusual form for a small ruin—three rectangular rooms in a row from east to west, with three more swinging in an arc to the north and east from the central one around a depression which presumably marked the location of a kiva.

I dug over all of the surface rooms, beginning with the first one of those that branched off to the north. This room had been used as a burial chamber. The bodies of three adults had been prepared for burial in the customary fashion and laid on the floor of the room accompanied by pottery vessels, as was usual. However, they were merely laid away, and were not covered with earth until windblown sand and plaster washed down from the walls accomplished the purpose. Pottery vessels were scattered about the floor to the extent that it was impossible to tell which belonged with a respective skeleton. The storm-laid strata were so intensely hard that the only way in which I could dig them without breakage of the pottery was to undermine the floor, then chip down very carefully the first few inches above.

These burials would seem to date from very near the end of occupation of the region. At Site 41, at the Aztec Ruin, and elsewhere, I have seen other instances in which the dead were laid in abandoned chambers and left to time and the elements for burial. The most obvious interpretation would seem to be that such death occurred when the communities were in dire circumstances suffering, probably from starvation and disease, so that those remaining had not time nor energy to complete the interments in normal fashion.

Dimensions: Height, 3¾ in. (9.4 cm.).
Maximum diameter, 4⅜ in. (11.1 cm.).
Type: Mesa Verde Black-on-white.
UCM No. 9396.

Comments: This assortment of vessels contains examples of two ceramic forms that are diagnostic of certain segments of the San Juan during Pueblo III, demonstrating the regional specialization that took place at that time.

The abrupt-shouldered, straight or slightly tapering tall-necked pitcher, with pronounced demarcation between neck and body, is called the Chaco type because of its abundance in ruins in Chaco Canyon, New Mexico, and in areas influenced by Chaco peoples in early Pueblo III. The mug is recognized as the typical Mesa Verde drinking vessel during late Pueblo III. It is one of the most distinctive Mesa Verde vessel shapes. As may be noted in the figure, the typical mug is flat-bottomed, smaller at the top than at the base, has straight or somewhat bulging inward-sloping walls, and a vertical loop handle nearly the height of the vessel attached to one side. Most handles are flat and strap-like; a few are oval to circular in cross section. Keyhole or T-shaped perforations occasionally were made in mug handles, and on rare instances life forms were modeled on them.

Other examples of tall-necked pitchers with rather pronounced difference between neck and body are shown in the bottom half of Figure 26. A complete view of the pitcher shown in the upper grouping, which Morris describes as "the most gracefully shaped pitcher that I have seen from the San Juan" (UCM No. 9340), also is included. Those depicted are:

UCM No.	Provenience	Type	Diameter
9515	Tohatchi Flats	?	3⅝ in (9.2 cm.)
9407	La Plata valley	Mancos B/W	6¾ in. (17.4 cm.)
9480	Chaco Canyon	Escavada B/W	4⅜ in. (11.1 cm.)
9337	Near Chaco Canyon	Escavada B/W	6¼ in. (16.1 cm.)
9340	Near Farmington	Gallup B/W	8¾ in. (19.8 cm.)
9434	La Plata valley	Mesa Verde B/W	5⅛ in. (13 cm.)
9439	Near Gallup	Chaco B/W	7 in. (17.7 cm.)
9336	Near Chaco Canyon	Chaco B/W	6⅞ in. (17.5 cm.)

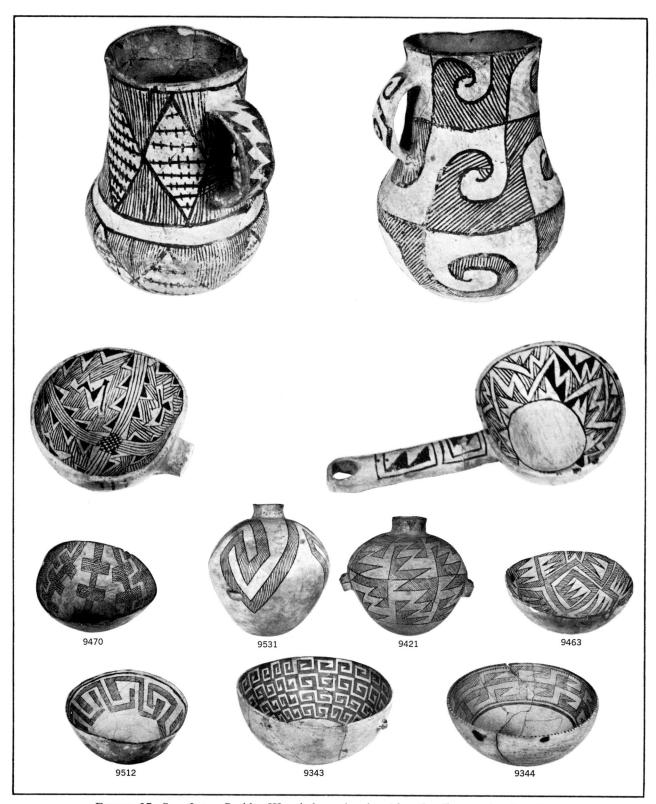

9470   9531   9421   9463

9512   9343   9344

Figure 27. San Juan, Pueblo III; pitchers, bowl-and-handle dippers, bowls, ollas, mostly Chaco Canyon style.

PUEBLO III

NAVAJO RESERVATION, NEW MEXICO (FIGURE 27)

(*Top left.*) Chaco pitcher, black-on-white. This and the three accompanying vessels from the Tohatchi Flats west of the Gallup-Shiprock highway, New Mexico.

Dimensions: Height, 6¾ in. (17.2 cm.).
Maximum diameter, 5 in. (12.8 cm.).
Type: Chaco Black-on-white (?).
UCM No. 9502.

(*Bottom left.*) Black-on-white dipper, handle broken.

Dimensions: Width of bowl, 5¾ in. (14.5 cm.).
Type: Tularosa Black-on-white, a type of pottery apparently made in the upper Little Colorado and Upper Gila areas, but which was traded into the San Juan area to the north. Some of its designs parallel those employed in the Chaco Canyon area.
UCM No. 9499.

(*Top right.*) Chaco pitcher, black-on-white.

Dimensions: Height, 7⅝ in. (19.5 cm.).
Maximum diameter, 5½ in. (14 cm.).
Type: Chaco Black-on-white.
UCM No. 9501.

(*Bottom right.*) Black-on-white dipper, rattle handle.

Dimensions: Length, 9⅜ in. (24 cm.).
Width of bowl, 5⅜ in. (13.7 cm.).
Type: Tularosa Black-on-white.
UCM No. 9500.

One day enroute to Gallup I picked up a Navajo boy who had a gunny sack in his hand. As he climbed into the car, the sack rattled, and I knew from the sound that it contained pottery. The boy said he was taking it to Gallup to sell. He was willing to guide me to the spot where he had found it, which lay some three miles west of the highway. It seemed that he had opened only the graves of which the slab covers were visible at the surface. I began scratching around in the spots between his pits, and in the course of two hours secured these specimens. This was in the summer of 1928.

Comments: In this figure, as well as in Figures 26 and 28, there are illustrated vessels from Pueblo III potters of Chaco culture. The climax of this development occurred in early Pueblo III; it centered in the numerous sites in and about Chaco Canyon, New Mexico, but has been found over much of the eastern San Juan area. Characteristic vessel shapes include: corrugated culinary pots, most frequently of the bell-mouthed variety hemispherical-shaped bowls, pitchers usually with an abrupt shoulder and a tall cylindrical neck, and bowl-and-handle dippers. Rarer forms are the cylindrical jar, the half-gourd ladle, pitchers with less distinction between neck and bottom, and effigy pots.

The decoration of Chaco black-on-white pottery includes band decorations that encircle the interiors of bowls. The bands may be made up of a repetition of identical units or of an alternation of two different units. Most bands are framed above and below by a single black line. Very characteristic of Chaco Canyon work is the use of lines dotted along one side. The spiral, frequently interlocking, in one form or another is also abundant, as is the ticked triangle. Large terraced elements are often outlined with a series of thin black lines. Hatching is perhaps the best earmark of Chaco art; the individual lines used are narrow and sometimes slightly wavy, and they almost always are framed in or enclosed by outer lines much heavier than themselves (Kidder, 1924: 52-53).

Most vessels in the lower section of Figure 27 also demonstrate characteristic Chaco Canyon patterns; however, specimens UCM No. 9343 and 9344 appear to have a combination of design elements found in both the Mesa Verde and Chaco Canyon areas. Those pictured are:

UCM No.	Provenience	Type	Diameter
9470	Gallup-Shiprock road	Gallup B/W	9½ in. (24.2 cm.)
9531	Newcombe's Post	Chaco B/W	15¼ in. (38.8 cm.)
9421	La Plata valley	Chaco B/W	11 in. (27.8 cm.)
9463	Newcombe's Post	Gallup B/W	10¼ in. (26.1 cm.)
9512	Tohatchi Flats	Chaco B/W	8⅝ in. (22 cm.)
9343	Near Aztec	McElmo B/W	12⅝ in. (32.2 cm.)
9344	Near Aztec	McElmo B/W	12 in. (30.6 cm.)

PUEBLO III

NAVAJO RESERVATION, ARIZONA-NEW MEXICO
(FIGURE 28)

(*Left rear.*) Large corrugated jar, unusual in all respects. It is very squat and wide mouthed in proportion to its height. The base is plain up to about two inches of the girdle; thence the corrugations are visible, but considerably wiped down, for about six inches, where they give way to a very wide outflaring rim. The color is mottled gray to pink. The vessel was brought to me in 1931 by a Navajo who found it weathered out of an open site somewhere along the valley leading into the Lukachukai Mountain in which the Cove Experiment Station was later to be constructed.

Dimensions: Height, 11¾ in. (29.9 cm.).
Maximum diameter, 13⅛ in. (33.4 cm.).
Type: Jeddito Corrugated. This type of pottery was indigenous to the Jeddito district of the northern Little Colorado drainage and is more characteristic of Pueblo IV. The form of this pot is not unusual for Jeddito Corrugated.
UCM No. 9447.

(*Middle rear.*) Huge black-on-white bowl, early Pueblo III. One-half restored. From the cluster of ruins known as the Bennett's Peak group lying near the Gallup-Shiprock road. The great bowl was among a collection of a hundred odd pieces that I gathered for the University of Colorado Museum in the summer of 1925. I struck a pit cut into natural soil under about a half foot of refuse. On the bottom of it lay the skeleton of an adult, on the right side, partially flexed, with head to the south. As I worked upward from the foot, I struck the edge of the great bowl opposite the breast, sitting as if complete; but as I dug around it, it soon became apparent that only half of it was present. The broken edges were jammed tight against the wall of the pit, and five other bowls were nested inside it. Because of the large size of the vessel and its striking pattern, I was disgusted beyond measure not to secure all of it. Years later I obtained it from the museum in exchange for other specimens, and had the missing half restored by Mrs. Myer.

Dimensions: Height, 6 in. (15.2 cm.).
Maximum diameter, 14¾ in. (37.5 cm.).
Type: Possibly Tularosa Black-on-white.
UCM No. 9553.

(*Right rear.*) Corrugated pot of about three quarts capacity. Globular in form, with neck about one inch in height, and flaring rim. Deeply indented up to girdle; relatively smooth coils thence to root of neck, which is coiled like the base. Two horizontal loop handles anchored a little way above the girdle. Brought into the Prayer Rock camp in 1931 by One-Eyed Moccasin Maker, who lived on the main branch of Black Horse Creek. Said to have been found in a cave in the southeast skirt of Carriso Mountain.

Dimensions: Height, 9¼ in. (23.5 cm.).
Maximum diameter, 9¼ in. (23.4 cm.).
Type: Tusayan Corrugated (?).
UCM No. 9452.

(*Left front.*) Hachured Chaco pitcher.
Dimensions: Height, 6½ in. (16.7 cm.).
Maximum diameter, 5¾ in. (14.5 cm.).
Type: Chaco Black-on-white.
UCM No. 9616.

(*Right front.*) Small corrugated pot. The very narrow spiral coil is deeply indented. An extremely fine example.
Dimensions: Height, 4¾ in. (12 cm.).
Maximum diameter, 4⅝ in. (11.6 cm.).
Type: Mesa Verde Corrugated.
UCM No. 9517.

One day in 1924 I drove off across the flats east of the highway about 3 miles south of the Naschidi Post, following Navajo wagon tracks when they went in a direction which suited me and cutting across country at other times. I located a number of small, widely scattered sites of early Pueblo III age. To judge from the meager refuse piles, they had been but briefly occupied. In the edge of a small gully cut through one of the heaps there were a few bones of the skeleton of an adult, accompanied by this corrugated pot and the hachured Chaco pitcher described above. As near as I could judge, this site was about 2½ miles east of the Gallup-Shiprock highway.

Comments: The corrugated cooking jars with egg-shaped bodies, mouths approximately half the maximum diameter of the vessel, and rims sharply everted, as shown in the lower part of Figure 28 are typical of most parts of the San Juan during late Pueblo III. Those pictured are:

UCM No.	Provenience	Type	Diameter
9437	La Plata valley	Mesa Verde Corrug.	5¼ in. (13.3 cm.)
9404	La Plata valley	Mesa Verde Corrug.	3⅞ in. (9.9 cm.)
9427	La Plata valley	Mesa Verde Corrug.	11⅝ in. (29.6 cm.)
9390	La Plata valley	Mesa Verde Corrug.	9¼ in. (23.6 cm.)
9353	Near Aztec Ruin	Mesa Verde Corrug.	11¾ in. (29.7 cm.)
9425	La Plata valley	Mesa Verde Corrug.	13⅝ in. (34.7 cm.)
9426	La Plata valley	Mesa Verde Corrug.	14¾ in. (37.5 cm.)
9378	Holmes Group	Mesa Verde Corrug.	15 in. (38.2 cm.)

9437   9404   9427   9390

9353   9425   9426   9378

FIGURE 28. San Juan, Pueblo III; corrugated jars, bowl, pitcher.

Pueblo III

Lower Animas Valley, New Mexico (Figure 29)

Large black-on-white, classic Mesa Verde mug. Rattle bottom. Partly restored. Found in shallow gully that runs from northwest to southeast back of the East Pueblo at Aztec Ruin. North of the west end of the eastern one of the two structures which compose the East Pueblo, there was a low mound which had the appearance of a trash heap. Where the gully had cut against this there was visible almost immediately below the surface, a layer indubitably representative of intentional cremation by a Mesa Verde group. Charred human bones, carbonized bits of feather-string cloth and plaited rush matting, and blackened potsherds gave ample indication that bodies had been prepared as customary for burial, laid upon the mound with usual accompaniments, then burned and the residue covered with refuse earth. I observed these conditions in 1925, at which time I picked up the mug above listed, but never found an opportunity to investigate this evidence of cremation further.

I am not certain in the matter, but it is my impression that during landscaping done under the Public Works Administration project of 1934 the trash pile was plowed over. If so, the stratum presenting evidence of cremation must have been hopelessly scrambled.

Dimensions: Height, 4⅞ in. (12.3 cm.).
Maximum diameter, 4⅛ in. (10.6 cm.).
Type: Mesa Verde Black-on-white.
UCM No. 9351.

Comments: The "rattle-bottomed" mug is rare but is nevertheless a definite type which may be expected in any locality where Mesa Verde pottery occurs. It was manufactured by forming a double bottom on the mug with sufficient space in the cavity to permit the inclusion of several balls of clay. Movement of the mug causes the pellets to rattle against the bottoms and walls of the vessel.

Cremation was not a usual form of disposal of the dead by the Anasazi. Inhumation of the corpse in refuse deposits, in abandoned habitations or storage units, and beneath the floors of rooms that continued to be occupied were common practices in the San Juan. Mortuary offerings were characteristic at all times.

Fourteen other examples of Mesa Verde mugs from the Morris Collection are shown to smaller scale in Figure 29. Those pictured are:

UCM No.	Provenience	Type	Diameter
9322	Near Farmington	McElmo B/W	2⅜ in. (6.3 cm.)
9349	Near Aztec Ruin	Mesa Verde B/W	3¾ in. (9.6 cm.)
9417	La Plata valley	Mesa Verde B/W (?)	2⅞ in. (7.3 cm.)
9333	Near Farmington	Mesa Verde B/W	4 in. (10.3 cm.)
9433	La Plata valley	Mesa Verde B/W	3¾ in. (9.5 cm.)
9397	La Plata valley	Mesa Verde B/W	3⅛ in. (7.9 cm.)
9332	La Plata valley	Mesa Verde B/W	3⅜ in. (8.8 cm.)
9432	La Plata valley	Mesa Verde B/W	3¾ in. (9.6 cm.)
9489	Ackmen, Colorado	Mesa Verde B/W	3¾ in. (9.4 cm.)
9443	Montezuma valley	Mesa Verde B/W	3⅛ in. (7.9 cm.)
9409	La Plata valley	Mesa Verde B/W	2 in. (5.1 cm.)
9401	La Plata valley	Mesa Verde B/W	3¼ in. (8.4 cm.)
9402	La Plata valley	Mesa Verde B/W	4 in. (10.1 cm.)
9465	San Juan valley	Mesa Verde B/W	3⅜ in. (8.6 cm.)

FIGURE 29. San Juan, Pueblo III; Mesa Verde mugs.

PUEBLO III

SAN JUAN VALLEY, NEW MEXICO (FIGURE 30)

(*Left rear.*) Mesa Verde bowl in classic style. Unusually fine workmanship. Found by Scott N. Morris on the Blake ranch, Farmington, spring of 1904.

Dimensions: Height, 3¼ in. (7.9 cm.).
Diameter at rim, 6⅞ in. (17.4 cm.).
Type: Mesa Verde Black-on-white.
UCM No. 9323.

(*Middle.*) Very large Mesa Verde bowl. Obtained by Earl Morris in 1934 from a cobblestone ruin near the Holmes Group in the lower La Plata valley. The bowl lay inverted over the skull of a very old person who had been laid away on the bottom of a jug-shaped storage pit that reached down 6 feet below the floor in the corner of a room.

Dimensions: Height, 5 in. (12.7 cm.).
Diameter at rim, 11⅞ in. (30 cm.).
Type: Mesa Verde Black-on-white.
UCM No. 9429.

(*Left front.*) Small Mesa Verde bowl. Intricate all-over black-on-white pattern on interior, exterior band pattern. Tiny eyelets on opposite sides just below rim. Superior example of classic Mesa Verde workmanship. Found by Albert Wooton in the winter of 1891 on the mesa point north of what was then the confluence of the Animas and San Juan Rivers. The old Negro came to Mother one morning and asked if he might borrow a shovel, saying that he had dreamed just where he could find something and wanted to go and dig it up. A while later he came back with this bowl, still filled with earth, in his hand. I still remember standing beside the gaunt old fellow and looking between the spread fingers of his hand at the bottom of the bowl as he handed it to Mother.

Dimensions: Height, 2½ in. (6.3 cm.).
Diameter at rim, 5¾ in. (14.6 cm.).
Type: Mesa Verde Black-on-white.
UCM No. 9304.

(*Right rear.*) Mesa Verde bowl. Butterfly pattern on exterior. This was found by Earl Morris in the Old Fort, south of the San Juan, opposite Farmington, spring of 1908. On a high school picnic for which my team furnished one of the principal units of transportation, I had along, as usual, a pick and shovel. In climbing up a slope about half way between the flat and the ledge cropping on which most of the ruins stands, I noticed a floor line showing at the surface. I began following this into the hill, but had gotten only a fair start by lunch time. After lunch the rest of the crowd set out to climb as far as they could toward the top of the cliff beyond the gully to the southwest. I decided to go on with my digging, and before long I had the company of the chaperon who was too bulky to follow the crowd in its scramblings. After a time I came upon a cavity in the earth and stone fill. Beneath it soft earth reached down below the level of the floor that I had been following. I thrust my shovel into it and brought up a number of human ribs. When finally I raveled out the situation, it proved that the floor was that of the deep southern recess of a kiva. The body of an adult had been shoved feet first into the ventilator shaft which ran southward beneath the recess, and to seal the mouth of the opening a stone slab had been set up against the wall. The body lay on the left side, facing east. The bowl set on edge with the open side against the sandstone east wall of the tunnel. The bottom touched the right cheek of the skull. Upright inside it was a mug, and just forward of these was a small corrugated pot of very fine workmanship. Among the mould around the bones were rotted cordage of a feather-string blanket and similiar vestiges of plaited rush matting. Long after the hill had assumed its present slope, the cedar lintels of the ventilator tunnel had given way, permitting the earth above to settle down around the bones, thus producing the cavity that so puzzled me when I first saw it.

Dimensions: Height, 3¼ in. (8.1 cm.).
Diameter at rim, 7¼ in. (18.5 cm.).
Type: Mesa Verde Black-on-white.
UCM No. 9334.

(*Right front.*) Small Mesa Verde bowl. Has a most unusual exterior decoration. From a black border just below the rim a crudely executed meander band crosses on the line of a diameter (the pattern is shown in Morris, 1939, figure 59, *27*). This vessel came from a sub-floor burial in the same ruin in the lower La Plata valley from which the very large Mesa Verde bowl shown in the middle of this illustration also was obtained.

Dimensions: Height, 2⅜ in. (6.2 cm.).
Diameter at rim, 5⅜ in. (13.5 cm.).
Type: Mesa Verde Black-on-white.
UCM No. 9431.

FIGURE 30. San Juan, Pueblo III; Mesa Verde bowls.

Comments: In Figures 26 and 29 through 36 there are examples of typical Mesa Verde pottery of the Pueblo III period from the Morris Collection. It occurs not only on the Mesa Verde proper, part of which has been set aside as Mesa Verde National Park, but over much of the San Juan drainage, especially in southwestern Colorado, northwestern New Mexico, and southeastern Utah. This ceramic complex reached its classic development and was distributed most widely in late Pueblo III.

The corrugated cooking jar moved from the bell-mouthed form toward the egg-shaped body with mouths only half the maximum diameter of the vessel and rims sharply everted. Other typical forms include: large, globular-bodied, short necked, handled water and storage jars; kiva jars, a globular vessel with an encircling rim about the orifice creating a flange well suited to support a disk-shaped lid of stone or pottery; bowls of varying size; mugs; and bowl-and-handle dippers. Less characteristic, but sometimes present are canteens, pitchers, and bird-form vessels.

The decoration of Mesa Verde Pueblo III black-on-white pottery is, with the exception of certain zoomorphic figures on bowl exteriors, almost strictly geometric. It is nevertheless bold and free. Large, striking elements are used, and the contrast between them and the clear, pearly-white vessel surface is very pleasing. The earmarks of Mesa Verde design are: the use of balanced sets of framing lines above and below band decorations, the prevalence of patterns, either continuous or of repeated units, on bowl exteriors, and the common occurrence of large designs in solid black and hatching which cover the entire interiors of bowls. Elements found principally in designs are well drawn lines, grading from moderately narrow to very broad, dots, triangles, terraces, checkerboards, and rarely life forms.

Bowls with squared rims decorated with black dots, or "ticks," such as are illustrated by these five vessels, are Mesa Verde hallmarks.

The remainder of the black-on-white bowls showing Mesa Verde Pueblo III designs are included in the lower portion of

Figure 30. Both McElmo Black-on-white and Mesa Verde Black-on-white types are represented, and the specimens exemplify the range of potters' skills apparent in a typical collection from sites in the San Juan. Both forms and techniques of decoration vary considerably, reflecting the abilities of individual artisans. Those pictured are:

UCM No.	Provenience	Type	Diameter
9382	La Plata valley	McElmo B/W	7½ in. (19.2 cm.)
9406	La Plata valley	McElmo B/W	12⅝ in. (32.1 cm.)
9405	La Plata valley	McElmo B/W (?)	12⅛ in. (30.9 cm.)
9324	Near Farmington	McElmo B/W (?)	12⅛ in. (30.7 cm.)
9535	Bennett's Peak	McElmo B/W	7⅛ in. (18.2 cm.)
9306	Unknown	Mesa Verde B/W	4⅛ in. (10.3 cm.)
9423	Holmes Group	Mesa Verde B/W	7 in. (17.7 cm.)
9430	La Plata valley	Mesa Verde B/W	7 in. (17.9 cm.)
9398	La Plata valley	Mesa Verde B/W	7⅜ in. (18.6 cm.)
9399	La Plata valley	Mesa Verde B/W	6¼ in. (15.7 cm.)
9422	Holmes Group	Mesa Verde B/W	8¼ in. (20.9 cm.)
9393	La Plata valley	Mesa Verde B/W	11½ in. (29.1 cm.)
9536	Newcombe's Post	Mesa Verde B/W (?)	7⅞ in. (20 cm.)
9400	La Plata valley	Mesa Verde B/W	5⅝ in. (14.2 cm.)
9355	Near Aztec Ruin	Mesa Verde B/W	6⅞ in. (17.6 cm.)
9394	La Plata valley	Mesa Verde B/W	7⅜ in. (18.8 cm.)
9356	Near Aztec Ruin	Mesa Verde B/W	12⅜ in. (31.3 cm.)
9392	Holmes Group	Mesa Verde B/W	10½ in. (26.6 cm.)

PUEBLO III

LA PLATA VALLEY, NEW MEXICO (FIGURE 31)

(*Left rear.*) Medium sized Mesa Verde bowl with a most unusual all-over black-on-white pattern. Found by P. T. Hudson at the Holmes Group, lower La Plata valley.

Dimensions: Height, 3⅝ in. (9 cm.).
Diameter at rim, 7⅝ in. (19.4 cm.).
Type: Mesa Verde Black-on-white.
UCM No. 9379.

(*Left front, middle.*) Mesa Verde black-on-white dipper with all-over scroll-at-center pattern (illustrated in Morris, 1939, plate 302w). Purchased from Tom Dosher in 1933. From a small ruin situated in the bottom of the first draw north of Site 41, lower La Plata valley.

Dimensions: Length, 9 in. (23.1 cm.).
Width of bowl, 3⅞ in. (9.8 cm.).
Type: Mesa Verde Black-on-white.
UCM No. 9383.

(*Front.*) Mesa Verde dipper, early Pueblo III. This specimen is extraordinary because of the length of the handle. Found in the Jewett valley and came into the possession of A. M. Amsden, of Farmington, soon after 1900. I first saw it in the collection he displayed in the window of his bank. Late in 1937 I saw the dipper, which I had always coveted, among the relics in a cabinet on the second floor of his hotel. With the thought that he might have changed his mind in the intervening years, I asked him if he would consider selling it, and to my great surprise he made me a present of it. One side of the bowl was missing, and the handle was somewhat chipped. The missing parts were restored by Mrs. Myer.

Dimensions: Length, 12¾ in. (31.9 cm.).
Width of bowl, 3 in. (7.7 cm.).
Type: Mesa Verde Black-on-white.
UCM No. 9478.

FIGURE 31. San Juan, Pueblo III; Mesa Verde bowl-and-handle dippers, bowl.

(*Right middle.*) Mesa Verde black-on-white dipper with all-over square-at-center pattern. Found by Earl Morris during the winter of 1930-31 in a small house mound near Site 41 in the lower La Plata valley.

Dimensions: Height, 2 in. (5.2 cm.).
 Length, 9⅛ in. (23.2 cm.).
 Width of bowl, 4¾ in. (12.1 cm.).
Type: Mesa Verde Black-on-white.
UCM No. 9395.

(*Right front.*) Small Mesa Verde black-on-white dipper. From a sub-floor burial in the long building across the low swale south of the great sandstone pueblo at Site 41, lower La Plata valley. This burial had been disturbed before the building had been abandoned, all but shreds of the bones and sherds of the vessels having been removed. Half the dipper was found in one end of the burial pit, the remainder at the other.

Dimensions: Length, 6 in. (15.2 cm.).
 Width of bowl, 3⅜ in. (8.6 cm.).
Type: Mesa Verde Black-on-white.
UCM No. 9413.

Comments: The four bowl-and-handle dippers in this group are distinctive of Pueblo III. Note both solid and hollow-cylindrical handles. Hollow handles sometimes had clay pellets in them which causes the dipper to rattle when it is moved. The length of the handle on the front dipper is unusually long.

Other bowl-and-handle dippers in the collection are depicted in the bottom section of Figure 31. The fragmentary specimens (UCM Nos. 9410, 9411) have similar spiral designs in the bowls. Those pictured are:

UCM No.	Provenience	Type	Diameter
9326	La Plata valley	Mancos B/W	7½ in. (18.9 cm.)
9418	La Plata valley	Mesa Verde B/W	8⅞ in. (22.5 cm.)
9410	La Plata valley	Mesa Verde B/W	4½ in. (11.6 cm.)
9411	La Plata valley	Mesa Verde B/W	3¾ in. (9.6 cm.)
9419	La Plata valley	McElmo B/W	8 in. (20.4 cm.)
9403	La Plata valley	Mesa Verde B/W	7½ in. (19 cm.)

PUEBLO III

SAN JUAN VALLEY, NEW MEXICO (FIGURE 32)

Large Mesa Verde olla. Found about 1905 by Bobby Smith on his ranch in the San Juan valley about 5 miles southeast from Farmington. I first saw this specimen at a fair in Farmington in 1906 or '07. Smith brought it in to exhibit beside some specimens that I had to display. I tried my best then and several times during the following years to purchase it from him, but he could not be persuaded to part with it. He had found it under rather unusual conditions. In looking for his cows one evening down in the river flat after the spring run-off had subsided, he saw the vessel lying bottom up in a pile of driftwood. Undoubtedly it had been covered with a flat stone so that no earth trickled inside. When dumped into the water by the caving of a bank, the spherical form of the body saved it from sinking and consequent destruction. The weight of the neck was sufficient to turn the sphere upside down, so that the vessel floated.

In the summer of 1913 I entered Pierce's store in Farmington and saw the jar sitting on the topmost shelf near the front of the building. I was much surprised and questioned Jim Pierce about it. He said that old Bobby had brought it there for safe-keeping because he was afraid it would get broken if it remained in his house. I found the old man on the street that day and again tried to make some sort of deal with him, but he was as obdurate as ever. Then I went back to Pierce's and asked Jim if Bobby owed him anything. He consulted his ledger and said, "Yes. Thirty-five dollars." I told him to get me the pot and I would pay the bill, and thus I came to be the owner.

I shrank from taking the specimen home because I knew the well-deserved lecture I would get from my mother for squandering so much money; so I made an agreement with Jim to leave the jar where it was until my return from school the next summer. In January of 1914 I made a second trip to Quirigua, Guatemala. While there a letter from Mother informed me that Pierce's store and all its contents had been destroyed by fire. Naturally I concluded that the large jar had gone with the rest. When I returned to Farmington in early summer, something took me into Harrington's bank, and there, sitting high on a partition between two of the cages, was old Bobby's olla. Who brought it out of the burning building and turned it over to Harrington, I was never able to learn. I told Harrington that it belonged to me, but he merely laughed at my claims. I did not press the matter, for I had long desired to change the looks of his face, and thought that if the argument became heated I would be pretty likely to try it. Later in the summer Jim Pierce returned to Farmington and went with me to recover the specimen from Harrington.

Dimensions: Height, 12½ in. (32.4 cm.).
 Maximum diameter, 13⅛ in. (33.2 cm.).
 Neck height, 2⅛ in. (5.3 cm.).
Type: Mesa Verde Black-on-white.
UCM No. 9330.

FIGURE 32. San Juan, Pueblo III; Mesa Verde olla.

Figure 33. San Juan, Pueblo III; Mesa Verde olla.

PUEBLO III

LA PLATA VALLEY, NEW MEXICO (FIGURE 33)

Unusually large Mesa Verde olla with elaborate square-at-center pattern (illustrated in Morris, 1939, plate 305b, b′). In the summer of 1934, while I was superintending repair work at Mesa Verde and at the Aztec Ruin, on several occasions I swung across country between the two places by way of the La Plata valley and stopped to dig for a few hours; and on three or four Sundays I drove over from Aztec for that purpose. I put in practically all of the time in one building—the first ruin south of the Prewitt pasture cut-off between Aztec and the La Plata, and just east of the lane which runs from north to south through the Holmes Group. The cobblestone building had consisted of an east-and-west range six rooms long and two wide, with a two room wing jutting south from the east end and another from the center. There was a kiva depression between these two wings and suggestion of another west of the western one. The refuse area and most of the wings had been previously dug, and a number of pits had been sunk in the main part of the house. I dug over all of the rest of it. Three large corrugated jars and this black-on-white olla had been buried as cache pots under the floors. Other pottery vessels, including two of the bowls in Figure 30, came from sub-floor burials elsewhere in the building.

Dimensions: Height, 13¾ in. (34.9 cm.).
Maximum diameter, 14¾ in. (37.4 cm.).
Neck height, 1⅞ in. (4.9 cm.).
Type: Mesa Verde Black-on-white.
UCM No. 9428.

9391   9328   9388

Figure 34. San Juan, Pueblo III; Mesa Verde ollas.

PUEBLO III

LA PLATA VALLEY, NEW MEXICO (FIGURE 34)

Large Mesa Verde olla (illustrated in Morris, 1939, plate 306a, a'). Found by Elmer Dosher at small ruin situated in the bottom of the first draw north of Site 41, lower La Plata valley. I first saw this in the summer of 1933 and tried to purchase it without results. In the fall of 1934 I drove up the La Plata valley to see if Dosher had changed his mind. It proved that he had moved into the Animas valley, above Cedar Hill, where I finally found him. This time he was willing enough to sell, and took me into a dugout cellar where we finally located a mouldy carton containing the fragments, partly buried by a pile of rotting potatoes. A few pieces of the vessel had been lost, but the missing places were filled out most satisfactorily by Mrs. Myer.

Dimensions: Height, 12¾ in. (32.4 cm.).
Maximum diameter, 12¾ in. (32.4 cm.).
Neck height, 2 in. (5 cm.).
Type: Mesa Verde Black-on-white.
UCM No. 9389.

Comments: Beneath the large olla are three other Mesa Verde ollas in the Morris Collection. Those pictured are:

UCM No.	Provenience	Type	Diameter
9391	La Plata valley	Mesa Verde B/W	11 in. (28 cm.)
9328	Near Farmington	Mesa Verde B/W	13 in. (32.5 cm.)
9388	La Plata valley	Mesa Verde B/W	12¼ in. (30.8 cm.)

PUEBLO III

LOWER ANIMAS VALLEY, NEW MEXICO (FIGURE 35)

(*Left.*) Very large black-on-white bowl, unbroken. The band pattern, characterized by a balance of hachured and solid elements, although not typical, is clearly of Mesa Verde character. This is confirmed by the finish of the vessel and by the flattened, dotted rim. Found by Sherman Howe on his property about ⅜ mile northeast of the Aztec Ruin. One afternoon he turned the waste water from a small irrigation ditch over the edge of a high bank bordering the swampy river bottom. When he returned the next morning, the stream of water had laid bare this and another bowl and part of the skeleton of an adult, with which they had been buried. Accompanying them was a good-sized, characterless black-on-white pitcher. These were found in the spring of 1934, and I acquired them in the summer of that year.

Dimensions: Height, 5½ in. (14 cm.).
Maximum diameter, 12⅛ in. (30.9 cm.).
Type: Mesa Verde Black-on-white.
UCM No. 9345.

(*Right.*) Black-on-white bowl, Mesa Verde. Extremely intricate all-over spiral-at-center pattern.

In the spring of 1922 when I was hanging on at Aztec Ruin with the hope that the American Museum might change its mind and decide to go on with the work there, between watching the property, endeavoring to give courteous treatment to the visitors who came, and devoting what time I could to notes and manuscript, occasionally I got fed up to the point where it seemed advisable to get away for an interval. On the Farmer ranch, which adjoins the Sherman Howe property on the north, there were a number of small cobblestone ruins with accompanying refuse areas. Local people had burrowed about in these for years, but there were a few areas that remained untouched. Several times I slipped away at day-light, spent a few hours digging there, and got back to the ruin before it was time to expect visitors. In the small refuse area not more than a foot in depth, just north of Sherman Howe's fence, I found this bowl or what remained of it, lying upside down on natural earth beside a few bones of a small child. The pattern of the vessel was so striking that I had it restored by Mrs. Alma Myer when she was doing her best work.

Dimensions: Height, 3⅞ in. (9.8 cm.).
Diameter at rim, 8⅞ in. (22.6 cm.).
Type: Mesa Verde Black-on-white.
UCM No. 9352.

FIGURE 35. San Juan, Pueblo III; Mesa Verde bowls.

(*Middle.*) Medium sized Mesa Verde bowl with all-over spiral-at-center pattern. From a small cobblestone house about 50 yards north of the east end of the Aztec Ruin. This ruin was completely leveled down by H. D. Abrams not long before the American Museum of Natural History began excavation of the great pueblo. Abrams' hired man was doing the grading. Abrams himself was accustomed to return each noon to his home in town for lunch. One day just before he left he said to the hired man, "We're getting down pretty close to the bottom of this ruin, so be very careful. If the plow turns out any pottery, stop without going any farther."

Abrams was late in getting back to the ranch that afternoon. The fellow was plowing when he did put in an appearance, and Abrams saw over a certain area halves and thirds of bowls on the crest of each ridge of turned earth. He gathered up a good many of these, then began working with shovel and trowel through the area of their occur-

rence. In two adjoining rooms of the structure there had been an astonishing cache of pottery vessels. How many had been smashed by the plow Abrams never attempted to estimate, but he did recover *86* unbroken vessels beneath the level which had been reached by the plow share. Most of these were bowls. They had been nested in inverted position, grading from small at the bottom to large at the top. In one corner there was a small bowl half full of arrow points over which another had been turned upside down as a cover. In a niche in the dividing wall between the two chambers there was a medium-sized corrugated pot into which one could have reached a hand from either room. The bowl here is from the cache. I secured it from Boyd Abrams in exchange for a Casas Grandes vessel about 1930.

Dimensions: Height, 3¼ in. (7.9 cm.).
Diameter at rim, 7½ in. (19.1 cm.).
Type: Mesa Verde Black-on-white.
UCM No. 9342.

FIGURE 36. San Juan, Pueblo III; Mesa Verde bowl, canteen, mug.

PUEBLO III

LOWER ANIMAS VALLEY, NEW MEXICO (FIGURE 36)

(*Left.*) Large Mesa Verde bowl. Interior and exterior band patterns. Thin and light, classic in form, finish, and decoration. This and another bowl were with the burial of an adult in the trash mound of a cobblestone ruin on the Farmer ranch adjacent to Aztec Ruin. The bowls lay in the bottom of an oval pit cut about three feet into natural soil. The bowls were by the breast. At a height of about two feet above the remains, the pit had been roofed with small cedar timbers laid across the shorter dimension. Inverted above these, over the center of the pit, were two large corrugated jars. There could be no doubt that the space beneath the timbers had been left as a cavity, because when the sticks failed their broken ends settled down to touch the bones. In the settling process the corrugated jars became so shattered that I made no attempt to repair them. One had contained several quarts of fine-grained, white clay.

Dimensions: Height, 4½ in. (11.3 cm.).
Diameter at rim, 10⅜ in. (26.4 cm.).
Type: Mesa Verde Black-on-white.
UCM No. 9354.

Comments: Morris points out elsewhere in his catalogue that the distinctive features of this type of burial are the roofing of the pit some distance above the remains and the placing of pottery vessels upon the roof. He describes two other burials in the same site where such conditions existed, but noted that this type of burial pit was uncommon in the Animas, San Juan, and La Plata valleys. However, he stated that pit burials roofed with poles or stone slabs upon which vessels were crushed—most frequently corrugated pots, but occasionally a black-on-white one—occurred not infrequently along the eastern foot of the Chuska Range south of the San Juan. These so commonly contained Mesa Verde pottery that Morris postulated that this was a Mesa Verde method of interment widespread, though not too commonly practiced, during Pueblo III.

To our knowledge this sort of roofed burial pit with associated pottery has not been demonstrated to be frequent on the Mesa Verde proper.

(*Right.*) Large black-on-white Mesa Verde mug with curvilinear pattern. Found in irrigation ditch just south of the retaining wall which parallels the front of the Aztec Ruin, spring of 1923.

Dimensions: Height, 4⅜ in. (11 cm.).
                Maximum diameter, 4¼ in. (10.8 cm.).
Type: Mesa Verde Black-on-white.
UCM No. 9350.

Comments: Anasazi occupation of the eastern San Juan terminated at the end of Pueblo III, about A. D. 1300. By that time the tendency of progressive conservatism in vessel forms that began in Pueblo II had reduced the variety of pottery shapes to only a half dozen. In the initial period, Basket Maker III, there was a rather surprising number of forms, and these by no means primitive or experimental. In Pueblo I, the pot makers ran riot and produced the greatest profusion of forms that was ever to be attained. Thereafter, in Pueblo II and Pueblo III, the increasing conservatism eliminated one shape of vessel after another until at the end of Pueblo III only the cooking pot, the kiva jar, mug, bowl-and-handle dipper, water jar, and the bowl were left.

(*Middle.*) Black-on-white Mesa Verde water jar. About two quarts capacity. Eyelet handles well up on body wall. Original bale, a thick, many-ply rope of yucca, still intact. Very fine all-over pattern.

From Room 193 of the Aztec Ruin. Sifting of the refuse in this room yielded a surprising quantity of black-on-white potsherds. These I left at my mother's house for more than a year, and she spent all of her spare time sorting them. It soon became apparent that there were considerable portions of a number of vessels that promised to be restorable. They were, for the most part, water jars and mugs which seemed to be the work of a single potter. From time to time I set up the fragments she assembled. The total number of vessels recovered I do not remember. These were turned over to the Aztec Ruin Museum, and the missing portions were restored by Mrs. Alma Adams Myer in 1934. The specimen here listed was the most intriguing of the lot because of its rope bale and the elusiveness of its fragments. Mother stayed with the search for bits of it long after everything else was given up. When finally I put together the more than 100 fragments she had recognized, the vessel was about two-thirds complete. I had it restored by Mrs. Myer and kept it as a token of my mother's perserverance.

Dimensions: Height, 7⅜ in. (18.6 cm.).
                Maximum diameter, 8⅛ in. (20.7 cm.).
                Neck height, 1⅛ in. (3 cm.).
Type: Mesa Verde Black-on-white.
UCM No. 9359.

Comments: This form of vessel could also be called a canteen.

PUEBLO III

MONTEZUMA VALLEY, COLORADO (FIGURE 37)

Bowl which presumably would be classified as McElmo ware. It deviates far from a true circle and has a flat strap bale across the top. It is unslipped and leaden gray in color, like so much of the pottery from Montezuma Valley. The pattern consists of a series of nested triangle units based upon the rim, the inner one solid black. The use of what would appear to have been a white slip clay as a pigment, in opposition to the normal black, renders this vessel unique as far as my observation goes. The flat handle, decorated with a black and white diamond pattern, was broken away, but the stubs at each end justified a restoration.

Found by one Randall, presumably not far from his home, which is 5 miles west of Ackmen, Colorado. The bowl was purchased from him, along with some other pottery, by W. D. Ewing, of Durango, who gave it to me.

Dimensions: Height, 3½ in. (8.9 cm.).
                Maximum diameter, 7½ in. (19 cm.).
Type: Mancos Black-on-white.
UCM No. 9490.

Comments: The flat handle on this bowl is not a common occurrence. Most bowls with strap handles resemble the specimen illustrated in the lower part of Figure 37 in having more curved bails. The lower vessel is described as follows:

UCM No.	Provenience	Type	Diameter
9309	Near Farmington	McElmo B/W	5¼ in. (13.4 cm.)

9309

FIGURE 37. San Juan, Pueblo III; handled bowls.

PUEBLO III

MONTEZUMA VALLEY, COLORADO (FIGURE 38)

(*Left.*) Black-on-red bowl.

Dimensions: Height, 5⅞ in. (15 cm.).
          Maximum diameter, 12 in. (30.6 cm.).
Type: Wingate Black-on-red. Characteristic of late Pueblo II-Pueblo III.
UCM No. 9632.

(*Right.*) Black-on-red bowl.

Dimensions: Height, 5⅛ in. (13.3 cm.).
          Maximum diameter, 11¼ in. (28.4 cm.).
Type: Wingate Black-on-red.
UCM No. 9633.

(*Middle.*) Black-on-red bowl.

Dimensions: Height, 6 in. (15.1 cm.).
          Maximum diameter, 13¼ in. (33.6 cm.).
Type: Wingate Black-on-red.
UCM No. 9631.

These three black-on-red bowls presumably should be classified as Wingate Black-on-red. They were found at a site on the Colorado-Utah line about 7 miles west of south from the Monument Ruin, which is about 20 miles southwest of Dove Creek, Colorado. In the summer of 1940 Bob Burgh and I drove over from Durango to visit Al Lancaster at his home near Pleasant View. Both of us had long desired to see the Wilson Ruin (name now changed to Monument Ruin), which had been purchased by Professor L. L. Leh of the University of Colorado. Al had never seen the place himself, so was glad enough to go along to guide us to the general locality.

When we knew that we could not be very far from our objective, we stopped at a ranch house to make inquiry. It turned out to be the home of a Mr. Reed who had sold the Wilson Ruin to Professor Leh. At the time, Reed was off in a distant field superintending bean planting. Mrs. Reed directed us how to reach the ruin, then showed us some pottery that it was obvious she desired to sell. The ten or a dozen pieces impressed me as leavings no one else had cared to acquire, because everyone of them was off-color or a misfit in some respect. Finally she asked me if I was interested in red pottery, which I distinctly was. She brought up from the celler a carton full of fragments that had been well used as a nesting place for mice. We poured the contents out on the floor of the porch, and Bob and I began sorting. It soon became apparent that the lot contained the major portions of three vessels and quite a few fragments of three more; yet we could not be certain whether any of them were sufficiently complete to be restored. After spending all the time we dared in sorting, we drove on to the Wilson Ruin, looked it over, and then went back to the ranch.

By that time Mr. Reed had returned. I asked where and under what conditions he had found the mass of red fragments; and when he had described the site, I told him that I would give him ten dollars for the lot, providing he would take me to the spot where they had been unearthed.

He climbed in the old Packard with us and took us about 7 miles slightly west of south, as nearly as I could judge direction among the thick timber. Most of the way we followed a wood road with turns and twists so sharp that I fully expected to tear the top off the Packard before we were through. Finally Reed told us to stop, and then led us a few hundred yards to the west across broken, cedar-covered country to a small masonry ruin with a shallow, but rather large, refuse area southeastward of it. The refuse area had been riddled by the aimless gophering of inexperienced pothunters. The story that Reed told us was that someone else had dug out the broken red vessels, discarded them because they were broken, and that he had gathered up the fragments. My belief is that he did the job himself. At any rate he showed us the pit in which they had been found. Lying on the bank at one end of it were a good many sherds that we recognized as belonging to the vessels that we had seen at Reed's house. Earth from the pit seemed to have been tossed in all directions from it. We turned an area about 12 feet and in all obtained enough fragments to fill the crown of my hat. These, added to what Reed had saved permitted the restoration. Three other vessels were less than one-third complete.

The site at which they were found, although built somewhat earlier, had been inhabited into full Mesa Verde time, and Reed stated that in the grave whence came the red vessels there was also a typical mug. The body had lain on natural soil above which the refuse was not more than a foot deep. It would appear that whoever dug into it had thrust his shovel directly into the mass of red vessels, probably already crushed by earth pressure, and had shoveled them out like so much gravel. It is to be assumed that these three vessels were complete at the time of burial, but that only portions of the other three were placed in the grave. The presence of so much red pottery in a single grave in a region where such ware is extremely scarce is a phenomenal occurrence. I have been told, however, of one instance in which eleven red vessels were found with one skeleton at some point in the west Montezuma valley, Colorado.

FIGURE 38. San Juan, Pueblo III; red ware bowls and pitcher traded into San Juan.

Comments: BOB BURGH: Robert F. Burgh worked in the field and in the laboratory with Earl and was a member of the University of Colorado Museum staff. Died in 1962. AL LAN-CASTER: James A. Lancaster, well known field archaeologist who worked with Morris and other Southwestern archaeologists, and who spent many years with the National Park Service. Now, part-time Research Archaeologist with the University of Colorado.

During late Pueblo II and Pueblo III times locally made red pottery was practically nonexistent in the eastern San Juan; instead red ware from the upper Little Colorado drainage to the south was commonly imported into the San Juan villages. Wingate Black-on-red and toward the end of Pueblo III St. Johns Polychrome, a black-on-red with the addition of white designs on the exterior, were two of the most widely distributed trade products in the Southwest. Not only did they spread into the San Juan country, but they also diffused east and south into a large part of western New Mexico.

The additional black-on-red vessels in the lower portion of Figure 38 are typed Wingate Black-on-red. Those in the upper row, as was the case with the three bowls in the upper part of the figure, were traded into San Juan communities. The vessels in the lower row are all from sites in the upper Little Colorado area, where it is presumed they were manufactured. Those pictured are:

UCM No.	Provenience	Type	Diameter
9346	La Plata valley	Wingate B/R	9¾ in. (24.7 cm.)
9313	Near Farmington	Wingate B/R	10¾ in. (27.4 cm.)
9467	Newcombe's Post	Wingate B/R	9⅛ in. (24.4 cm.)
9639	Apache County, Arizona	Wingate B/R	13⅜ in. (34.2 cm.)
9637	Apache County, Arizona	Wingate B/R	9 in. (23 cm.)
9641	Apache County, Arizona	Wingate B/R	6½ in. (16.7 cm.)
9640	Apache County, Arizona	Wingate B/R (?)	9⅛ in. (23.4 cm.)
9636	Apache County, Arizona	Wingate B/R	12¾ in. (32.4 cm.)

FIGURE 39. San Juan, Pueblo III; polychrome bowls traded into San Juan.

PUEBLO III

LOWER ANIMAS VALLEY, NEW MEXICO (FIGURE 39)

(*Left, interior and exterior views.*) St. Johns Polychrome bowl. This was found in the lot now occupied by the Kiva Garage, which faces the Durango-Farmington highway from the south, three-quarters of a block west of the main north and south street of Aztec, New Mexico. One morning in the winter of 1922-23 as I was driving from the ruin into Aztec for mail, I noticed the heads of two men showing above a small mound of fresh earth in the vacant lot. One was an old acquaintance, A. B. Hardin; the other, C. E. Rippey, owner of the residence on the next lot to the west. Hardin beckoned me over. It proved that Rippey, while digging a trench for a gas pipe, had struck a burial about 15 inches beneath the surface. He had little idea how to go about uncovering it, so I took over the job. In addition to the polychrome bowl, the skeleton of a young adult was accompanied by three black-on-white bowls— one large, one medium, one small—and a mug, all of typical Mesa Verde ware.

I did my best to talk Rippey out of this unusually fine polychrome, but he would neither trade nor sell. I kept track of the specimen, and a while after Rippey's death I

sent Ann around to the widow with the plan that she wanted to buy the bowl as a Christmas present for me because she thought there was nothing else that I would treasure as much.

Dimensions: Height, 4¼ in. (11 cm.).
　　　　　　　Maximum diameter, 9¾ in. (25 cm.).
Type: Wingate Polychrome; a type closely related to St. Johns Polychrome, but distinguished from it by having exterior designs in red instead of white.
UCM No. 9347.

NAVAJO RESERVATION, NEW MEXICO (FIGURE 39)

(*Right, interior and exterior views.*) St. Johns Polychrome bowl. From a site in the Tohatchi Flats, west of the Gallup-Shiprock highway, summer of 1928.

Dimensions: Height, 4¼ in. (10.8 cm.).
　　　　　　　Maximum diameter, 8¼ in. (21 cm.).
Type: St. Johns Polychrome.
UCM No. 9498.

9454

9491

9446   9657   9538   9337   9336

Figure 40. San Juan, Pueblo III; red ware pitchers, effigy figures on mug and pitcher handles.

PUEBLO III

SAN JUAN VALLEY, NEW MEXICO (FIGURE 40)

(*Left.*) Black-on-red pitcher. This is a representative of the red ware, which, when it has white or cream decoration in addition to the black, is called St. Johns Polychrome. It was found by the Brown brothers on their ranch east of Farmington in the winter of 1891 and '92. It was in a collection sold by my father to Gilbert McClurg. Being an unusual specimen, my mother retained a vivid memory of it and described it to me in such detail that I had no trouble picking it out when I saw it in the collection in Colorado Springs about 1935. I had gone there to lecture at the Taylor Museum. When ready to start back home, Mitchell Wilder, Director of the Museum, presented me with the piece.

Dimensions: Height, 6⅞ in. (17.1 cm.)
Maximum diameter, 5¾ in. (14.6 cm.).
Type: Difficult to classify. May be a poor example of Wingate Black-on-red, but temper may place into Tsegi Orange Ware. UCM No. 9310.

MESA VERDE, COLORADO (FIGURE 40)

(*Right.*) Black-on-red pitcher. It is as baffling a specimen to place as I have ever seen. It is of Chaco shape, but the design is not typical of anything with which I am familiar. The ground color is extremely dark, rich red; the decoration, a vivid black. It is the most lustrous prehistoric vessel that I have ever seen, due probably to the fact that it retains the polish and patina of use which has been removed by decay and leaching from all specimens that have been buried in earth that was even faintly moist. From Step House, Mesa Verde. I purchased this specimen from the widow of J. A. Jeancon. Written on the bottom is, "#4, Jeancon, 1908," and there is a label on which is written "S.W. Colorado." Long ago I admired this specimen in Jeancon's office, and he told me the circumstances of its finding. While on Mesa Verde in 1908, he was climbing up the slope of debris bordering the masonry structure in the north half of the cave when some stones gave way under his feet to cause quite a slide. When the debris cleared away, he spied, in the new surface, one side of this pitcher.

Dimensions: Height, 6¼ in. (15.9 cm.).
Maximum diameter, 4⅝ in. (11.9 cm.).
Type: Puerco Black-on-red, a variety of Wingate Black-on-red. UCM No. 9441.

Comments: Below the pitchers described above, and depicted in smaller scale, are two other Pueblo III black-on-red pitchers from the collection. The one on the left (UCM No. 9454) is not a normal form. The bottom row of Figure 40 shows five examples of modeled animal figures affixed to black-on-white pitcher or mug handles. The two pitchers are:

UCM No.	Provenience	Type	Diameter
9454	Canyon de Chelly	Tsegi Orange Ware	3½ in. (9 cm.)
9491	Flagstaff	Puerco B/R	8⅛ in. (20.7 cm.)

The bird effigy on UCM No. 9446 is 1¾ in. (4.5 cm.) long.

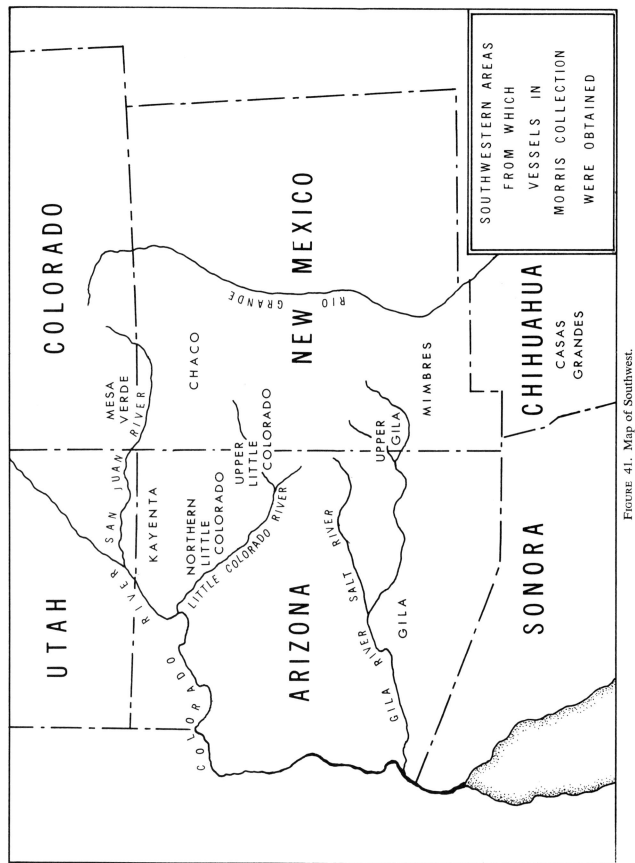

Figure 41. Map of Southwest.

FIGURE 42. Little Colorado, Pueblo III-IV; polychrome bowls.

PUEBLO III-IV

UPPER LITTLE COLORADO, ARIZONA (FIGURE 42)

Comments: These three vessels are examples of upper Little Colorado River drainage pottery from the area of their manufacture. They, and a few others from the same region, were obtained by Morris from the Field Museum of Natural History, Chicago, in exchange for a small collection of Basket Maker and Pueblo pottery from the Mesa Verde area. These related types represent points on a developmental continuum. The

St. Johns Polychrome bowl (UCM No. 9638) was made in Pueblo III; the two Four Mile Polychrome bowls (UCM nos. 9634 and 9635) represent a type that evolved in Pueblo IV.

UCM No.	Provenience	Type	Diameter
9638	Apache County, Arizona	St. Johns Poly.	13¼ in. (33.5 cm.)
9634	Homolobi, Arizona	Four Mile Poly.	11⅜ in. (28.8 cm.)
9635	Apache County, Arizona	Four Mile Poly.	8⅞ in. (22.8 cm.)

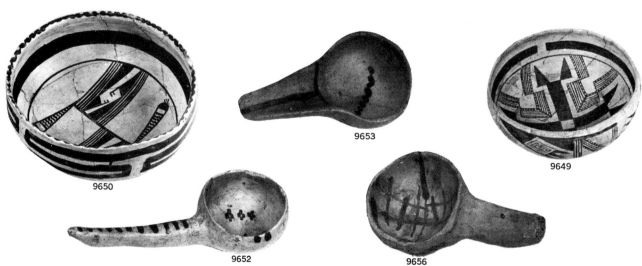

9650

9653

9649

9652

9656

FIGURE 43. Little Colorado, Pueblo IV; bowls and dippers.

PUEBLO IV

HOPI AREA, NORTHERN LITTLE COLORADO, ARIZONA
(FIGURE 43)

(*Left.*) Bowl, Jeddito Yellow.

Dimensions: Height, 3 in. (7.8 cm.).
Maximum diameter, 7⅛ in. (18.3 cm.).
Type: Jeddito Black-on-yellow.
UCM No. 9651.

(*Middle.*) Bowl, Sikyatki Polychrome.

Dimensions: Height, 3⅜ in. (8.9 cm.).
Maximum diameter, 8 in. (20.1 cm.).
Type: Sikyatki Polychrome.
UCM No. 9648.

(*Right.*) Large bowl, Sikyatki Polychrome. These three bowls are from the Hopi ruin of Kawaikuh, 1928.

Dimensions: Height, 4 in. (10.3 cm.).
Maximum diameter, 10⅞ in. (27.6 cm.).
Type: Sikyatki Polychrome.
UCM No. 9646.

Comments: The bottom section of Figure 43 illustrates additional Jeddito Black-on-yellow bowls and dippers in the Morris Collection. Those pictured are:

UCM No.	Provenience	Type	Diameter
9650	Kawaikuh	Jeddito B/Y	7 in. (17.8 cm.)
9653	Kawaikuh	Jeddito B/Y	3⅞ in. (9.8 cm.)
9649	Kawaikuh	Jeddito B/Y	9 in. (22.7 cm.)
9652	Kawaikuh	Jeddito B/Y	5¾ in. (14.6 cm.)
9656	Walpi	Jeddito B/Y (?)	4 in. (10 cm.)

PUEBLO IV

HOPI AREA, NORTHERN LITTLE COLORADO, ARIZONA
(FIGURE 44)

(*Left.*) Squat jar, Sikyatki Polychrome. I purchased this jar in Walpi in the summer of 1920, when I was on a reconnaissance expedition with Neil Judd. I had bought two large, old modern jars and then inquired from the several women standing about if they had any old pottery that had come from the ruins. One said that she had two broken pieces that her husband had found in old Sikyatki and had brought home so that she could copy the patterns. Because they were broken, I got them for a quarter. This is one of them. While we were bargaining, a little girl some three or four years old stepped up with a miserable dipper and said, "Fifteen cents, please;" I did not disappoint her.

Dimensions: Height, 6½ in. (16.7 cm.).
Maximum diameter, 11¼ in. (28.7 cm.).
Type: Sikyatki Polychrome.
UCM No. 9654.

(*Right.*) Large jar, Sikyatki Polychrome. From Awatovi. On several visits to the Peabody Museum camp at Awatovi, I slipped off to Kawaikuh for a few hours' digging and each time brought back and turned over to Jo Brew a number of pottery vessels. He promised that when the study of the collections was finished, he would send me as fine a jar and bowl as had been found at Awatovi. This is the jar he selected.

Dimensions: Height, 9⅛ in. (23.1 cm.).
Maximum diameter, 13⅞ in. (35.4 cm.).
Type: Sikyatki Polychrome.
UCM No. 9661.

Comments: NEIL JUDD: Southwestern archaeologist who worked many years for the Bureau of American Ethnology, the Smithsonian Institution, and the National Geographic Society. JO BREW: John Otis Brew, Director of the Peabody Museum, Harvard University, for almost twenty years. Other Sikyatki Polychrome bowls are shown in the lower part of Figure 44. The "miserable dipper" for which Morris paid fifteen cents is shown in Figure 43, UCM No. 9656. Those pictured in Figure 44 are:

UCM No.	Provenience	Type	Diameter
9662	Kawaikuh	Sikyatki Poly.	9⅞ in. (25 cm.)
9645	Kawaikuh	Sikyatki Poly.	13⅛ in. (33.3 cm.)
9655	Walpi	Sikyatki Poly.	8⅛ in. (20.6 cm.)
9647	Kawaikuh	Sikyatki Poly.	8½ in. (21.5 cm.)

9662

9647

9645

9655

FIGURE 44. Little Colorado, Pueblo IV; jars and bowls.

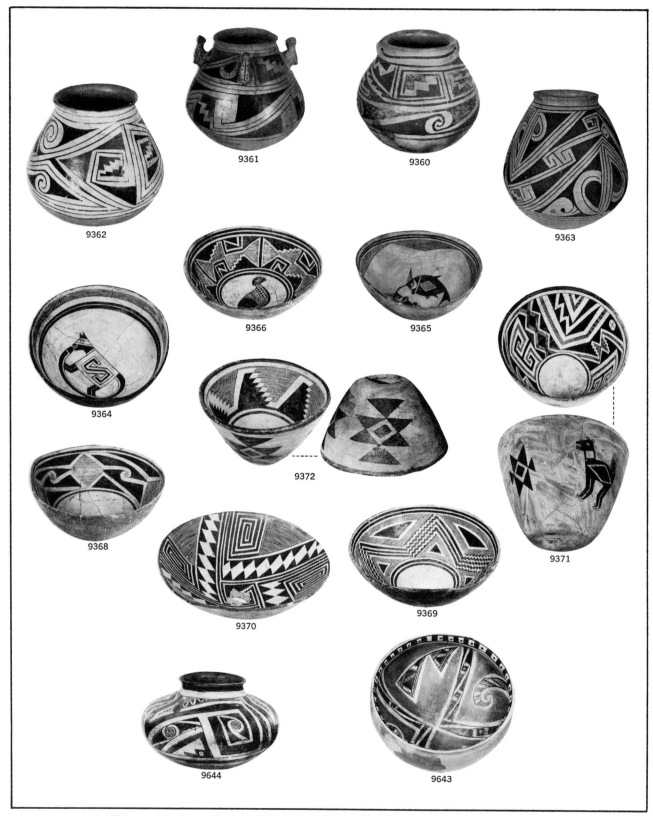

FIGURE 45. Casas Grandes, Mimbres, Middle Gila, Pueblo III-IV; jars, ollas, bowls.

Comments: The upper four polychrome jars (UCM nos. 9360, 9361, 9362, and 9363) are from the Casas Grandes area of northwestern Chihuahua, Mexico, and are of Pueblo IV age. Morris secured three of these in exchange for other pots from a collector in El Paso, Texas, in 1919, and the other in exchange from the Laboratory of Anthropology, Santa Fe, New Mexico, in 1936.

The polychrome olla (UCM No. 9644) and bowl (UCM No. 9643) at the bottom of Figure 45 are exemplary of Gila polychrome vessels made in the middle Gila drainage in Pueblo IV times. Morris obtained these from a site on the east side of the Gila River, about 3 miles above Safford, Arizona, summer of 1926.

The remaining eight bowls in the center of Figure 45 are from the Mimbres drainage of southwestern New Mexico. The group includes examples of both the excellent geometric and naturalistic black-on-white decorations employed by Mimbres potters during Pueblo III. It is some of the best design work in the prehistoric Southwest. Two of the bowls (UCM nos. 9370 and 9372) demonstrate the practice of knocking a small hole in the bottom of vessels when they were used as grave furnishings. Perhaps this custom was followed in order to free the spirit of the pot so that it could accompany the spirit of the person with whom it was buried. Earl Morris excavated these specimens from the Eby Ruin for the University of Colorado Museum in 1926. Later he obtained them by exchange with Professor Junius Henderson, curator of the Museum.

UCM No.	Provenience	Type	Diameter
9362	Casas Grandes, Mexico	Ramos Poly.	9½ in. (24.3 cm.)
9361	Casas Grandes, Mexico	Ramos Poly.	8⅝ in. (22.1 cm.)
9360	Casas Grandes, Mexico	Babicora Poly.	7¾ in. (19.9 cm.)
9363	Casas Grandes, Mexico	Ramos Poly.	8¼ in. (21.2 cm.)
9364	Mimbres, New Mexico	Mimbres B/W	9⅝ in. (24.6 cm.)
9366	Mimbres, New Mexico	Mimbres B/W	11 in. (27.8 cm.)
9365	Mimbres, New Mexico	Mimbres B/W	11⅞ in. (30.2 cm.)
9371	Mimbres, New Mexico	Mimbres B/W	9⅜ in. (23.8 cm.)
9372	Mimbres, New Mexico	Mimbres B/W	7⅜ in. (18.7 cm.)
9368	Mimbres, New Mexico	Mimbres B/W	12⅜ in. (31.4 cm.)
9370	Mimbres, New Mexico	Mimbres Bold Face B/W	10¾ in. (27.3 cm.)
9369	Mimbres, New Mexico	Mimbres B/W	10½ in. (26.7 cm.)
9644	Near Safford, Arizona	Gila Poly.	16½ in. (41.9 cm.)
9643	Near Safford, Arizona	Gila Poly.	10⅜ in. (26.3 cm.)

MINIATURE SPECIMENS

FIGURE 46. San Juan; miniature vessels.

Comments: Earl Morris had 77 miniature vessels in his private collection. Some were obtained through excavation, but the majority were given to him by or purchased from Navajo Indians, were gifts from trading post operators who had gotten them from Indians, or were collected through trade with museums and private collectors. A large assortment of these intriguing specimens is illustrated in Figure 46. The plain gray jar in the lower left of the figure is 2⅝ in. (6.7 cm.) high and 2⅛ in. (5.3 cm.) in diameter. It may serve as a scale for other vessels in the figure. Many of the miniatures are fairly accurate replicas of typical normal-sized vessels and their form and decoration allow them to be fairly positively identified as to time and place of manufacture. Others, however, are so characterless that they cannot be classified. A few are of historic Navajo manufacture. They vary from well-executed specimens, neatly formed and carefully decorated, to extremely crude examples apparently produced by children or inexperienced potters. Shapes include jars, pitchers, bowls, canteens, bird-shaped pots, mugs, and ladles or dippers, and appear to range from Basket Maker III to Pueblo III times.

BIBLIOGRAPHY

ABEL, LELAND J.
1955 "Pottery Types of the Southwest." *Museum of Northern Arizona Ceramic Series*, No. 3B. Flagstaff.

COLTON, HAROLD S.
1955 "Pottery Types of the Southwest." *Museum of Northern Arizona Ceramic Series*, No. 3A. Flagstaff.
1956 "Pottery Types of the Southwest." *Museum of Northern Arizona Ceramic Series*, No. 3C. Flagstaff.

HAYES, ALDEN C.
1964 "The Archeological Survey of Wetherill Mesa, Mesa Verde National Park, Colorado." *Archeological Research Series National Park Service*, No. 7-A. Washington.

KIDDER, A. V.
1924 "An Introduction to the Study of Southwestern Archaeology." *Papers Phillips Academy*, Southwestern Expedition, No. 1. Andover.

LAMBERT, MARJORIE F.
1966 "A Unique Kokopelli Jar." *El Palacio*, 72, No. 2. Santa Fe.

LISTER, FLORENCE C. and ROBERT H. LISTER
1968 "Earl Morris and Southwestern Archaeology." University of New Mexico Press. Albuquerque.

LISTER, ROBERT H.
1964 "Contributions to Mesa Verde Archaeology: I, Site 499, Mesa Verde National Park, Colorado." *Series in Anthropology University of Colorado Studies*, No. 9. Boulder.
1965 "Contributions to Mesa Verde Archaeology: II, Site 875, Mesa Verde National Park, Colorado." *Series in Anthropology University of Colorado Studies*, No. 11. Boulder.
1966 "Contributions to Mesa Verde Archaeology: III, Site 866 and the Cultural Sequence at Four Villages in the Far View Group, Mesa Verde National Park, Colorado." *Series in Anthropology University of Colorado Studies*, No. 12 Boulder.

LISTER, ROBERT H. and FLORENCE C. LISTER
1961 "The Coombs Site, Part III, Summary and Conclusions." *Anthropological Papers University of Utah*, No. 41. Salt Lake City.

MORRIS, EARL H.
1917 "Discoveries at the Aztec Ruin." *American Museum Journal*, 17, No. 3. New York.
1919 "Preliminary Account of the Antiquities of the Region between the Mancos and La Plata Rivers in Southwestern Colorado." *Thirty-Third Annual Report, Bureau of American Ethnology*. Washington.
1927 "The Beginnings of Pottery Making in the San Juan Area, Unfired Prototypes and the Wares of the Earliest Ceramic Period." *Anthropological Papers American Museum of Natural History*, 28, Pt. 2. New York.
1939 "Archaeological Studies in the La Plata District, Southwestern Colorado and Northwestern New Mexico." *Carnegie Institution of Washington*, Publication 519. Washington.

RODECK, HUGO G.
1956 "Earl Morris and the University of Colorado Museum, An Appreciation." *Southwestern Lore*, 22, No. 3. Boulder.

ROHN, ARTHUR H.
1959 "A Tentative Classification of Pottery from the Mesa Verde Region." Mimeographed. Mesa Verde National Park.